CGP

11+ Practice Paper

For Ages 10-11

Set A: Paper 1

For the CEM Test

Read the following:

Do not open this booklet or start the test until you are told to do so.

1. This test can be taken in either multiple-choice or write-in format.

2. If you are taking it as a multiple-choice test, you should mark your answer to each question in pencil on the separate answer sheet. Mark the correct box quickly and neatly using a horizontal line.

3. If you are taking it as a write-in test, you should write your answer to each question in pencil on the paper. Write your answer carefully in the space provided or, if there is a range of options, mark the correct box quickly and neatly using a horizontal line.

4. If you make a mistake, rub it out and mark your new answer clearly.

5. There are six sections in this test.

6. The time allowed for each section is given at the start of that section. You will have a total of 45 minutes to complete the timed sections of the test.

7. Each section includes examples showing you how to answer the questions. You may refer to these examples at any time as you work through the section.

8. Do as many questions as you can. For some questions you will be given a range of options — if you get stuck on one of these questions, choose the answer that you think is most likely to be correct, then move on to the next question. If you get stuck on a question for which no options are given, leave it and move on to the next question. If you have time at the end of the section, go back and have another go at the questions you could not answer.

9. You should do any rough working on a separate piece of paper.

Work carefully, but go as quickly as you can.

Section 1: Verbal Reasoning — Comprehension 1

Example Read these example questions. You may return to these examples at any time as you work through this section.

HMS Iolaire — A Tragedy Follows a Victory

1   World War I had just ended, the Armistice had been agreed, and a large number of sailors were making their way home to Stornoway on the island of Lewis, off the west coast of Scotland. They were looking forward to coming home.

     However, in the early hours of January 1st, 1919, disaster struck. HMS Iolaire
5   crashed into the notorious 'Beasts of Holm', a set of rocks just a mile away from the safety of Stornoway harbour. Around 50 men jumped overboard, planning to swim the short distance to the shore. Sadly, the stormy seas and windy conditions meant that these men perished. Meanwhile, there were many fatalities on board as the ship began to sink. The alarm was raised and the town's coastguard was called out, but by
10   the time he and his team arrived at the scene of the disaster, the ship had sunk.

A   Why did the sailors have to travel to Stornoway by boat?

- ☐ **A**   Because Stornoway is on the west coast of Scotland
- ☐ **B**   Because they were on their way back from World War I
- ■ **C**   Because Stornoway is on an island
- ☐ **D**   Because the 'Beasts of Holm' were dangerous

B   The 'Beasts of Holm' are described as "notorious" (line 5). What is meant by this?

- ☐ **A**   The rocks were concealed from view.
- ■ **B**   The rocks were well known for being dangerous.
- ☐ **C**   Many people admired the rocks.
- ☐ **D**   The rocks had a mysterious reputation.

End of example questions

 Wait until you are told to go on

You have 12 minutes to complete this section

There are 16 questions in this section

Read the passage carefully and then answer the questions that follow.

Don't get in a spin — cycling's for everyone

1   These days, we spend so much time sitting at desks and computers that it can be difficult to make time for exercise. But like it or not, getting exercise is a vital part of looking after your health. If you find it hard to drag yourself out for a run in the pouring rain, cycling could be the sport for you.

5   Riding a bike is one of the easiest ways to build regular exercise into your routine because it is also a way of getting around. You can exercise just by riding to work or school instead of travelling by car (and let's face it, there would be serious environmental benefits if more of us chose pedal power over fumy engines). Regular cycling will help you to lose weight, improve your fitness and reduce stress. It's a great way to exercise

10   without risking long-term injuries too: cycling puts very little strain on ankle, hip and knee joints (compared to high-impact sports such as running).

     As well as being good for you, cycling can be a lot of fun. Some people just enjoy getting out on a bike as a hobby, while for others it's a way of life. There are lots of different types of cycling to choose from, and some people choose them all!

15   **Road Cycling**

     Road cycling is one of the most popular sports in the UK. It's accessible to anyone as there are plenty of roads to choose from in the UK! You can ride any type of bike on the road, but people who take road cycling seriously use bikes that are very light with thin, smooth tyres to reduce friction. Road bikes often have curved handlebars so riders can

20   crouch down when they want to go faster. They have low gears for climbing up hills and high gears for riding fast on the flat or down hills.

     You've probably heard of the Tour de France, the most famous road cycling race in the world. Cyclists race for 21 days (with a couple of rest days on top of this) and ride up to 3500 kilometres.

25   **Mountain Biking**

     This involves riding off-road on tracks over moorland, hills, mountains and in forests. The UK is a great place to go mountain biking, with bridleways open to cyclists all over the country. There are popular and challenging routes in the national parks, such as the Lake District and Peak District. There are also trail centres with long tracks built exclusively for

30   mountain bikers. The varying difficulty of the trails is colour-coded: green is for easy, blue is for moderately hard, red is for difficult and black is for extremely difficult trails.

Passage continues over the page

Track Cycling

Track cycling is all about racing. It's done on a steeply banked track in an oval-shaped arena called a velodrome. There are a few velodromes around the UK, and
35 when professional races aren't being held, sessions at the tracks can be booked by anyone who wants to have a go. Track cycling events are a significant part of the Olympic Games with medals up for grabs for the most talented cyclists.

Track bikes are similar to road bikes, but they have only one gear and no brakes!

BMX

40 BMX (which stands for bicycle motocross) riding is also all about racing. Riders compete side-by-side (usually eight at a time) on a purpose-built dirt track with jumps and banked corners to see who can win a race over a single lap of the track. BMX bikes have raised handlebars, a single gear, and smaller wheels and frames than other bikes. BMX racing has grown in popularity in recent years, and in 2008 it featured in the Olympic
45 Games for the first time.

If any of this sounds interesting, then maybe cycling is something you should try. It's a sport that's accessible to everyone — whether you're old, young, able-bodied or disabled. Who knows? Maybe you could be a future winner of the Tour de France.

———————————

Answer these questions about the text. You can refer back to the text if you need to. Pick the best answer and draw a line through the rectangle next to it.

1 According to the text, which of these statements is false?

- A Track bikes only have one gear.
- B Track bikes have thin tyres.
- C Track bikes have straight handlebars.
- D Track bikes don't have brakes.

2 According to the text, how long does the Tour de France last?

- A One week
- B Less than three weeks
- C More than three weeks
- D A month

3 What does the author say is the main benefit of cycling?

- A It's good for the environment.
- B It's good for your health.
- C There are different types of cycling to choose from.
- D It puts very little strain on your joints.

4 According to the text, which of these statements is false?

- A Cycling can help keep you fit.
- B Anyone can ride in UK velodromes.
- C Track bikes have high gears for riding fast.
- D BMX bikes have raised handlebars.

5 Why does the author use the word "drag" (line 3)?

- A Because most people only go running if they are forced to.
- B To describe how you move your feet when you don't want to go running.
- C Because the author doesn't like running.
- D To emphasise that it can be difficult to make yourself go running.

Go to the next question

6 According to the text, why doesn't cycling cause many long-term injuries?

- ☐ A Because it only puts strain on your ankles, hips and knees.
- ☐ B Because you don't crash very often.
- ☐ C Because it doesn't put much strain on your joints.
- ☐ D Because it's a high-impact sport.

7 According to the text, which of these statements is true?

- ☐ A Road bikes have more gears than BMX bikes.
- ☐ B Road bikes are very heavy.
- ☐ C Road bikes have powerful brakes.
- ☐ D Road bikes only have one gear.

8 According to the text, why might a lot of people not get enough exercise?

- ☐ A They have busy lifestyles.
- ☐ B They don't like to run in the rain.
- ☐ C They prefer to travel by car.
- ☐ D They don't want long-term injuries.

9 Which two of the following are reasons why cycling is good for your health?

1) It improves your fitness.
2) You can do it while it's raining.
3) It's a good way of getting around.
4) It helps to reduce stress.

- ☐ A 2 and 4
- ☐ B 1 and 4
- ☐ C 1 and 3
- ☐ D 2 and 3

10 Which of the following does the author give as a disadvantage of running?

- ☐ A You can't run to work or school.
- ☐ B It's a low-impact sport.
- ☐ C It can cause long-term injuries.
- ☐ D It doesn't help you to lose weight.

11 Why do road bikes have thin tyres?

- ☐ A To look more professional.
- ☐ B To help them move faster.
- ☐ C To make them lighter.
- ☐ D To support lower gears.

12 The author uses the phrase "professional races" (line 35). This means races that:

　　A competitors volunteer for.
　　B competitors pay to take part in.
　　C competitors do very well in.
　　D competitors do to earn a living.

13 What does the word "exclusively" (line 29) mean?

　　A Mostly
　　B Privately
　　C Solely
　　D Partially

14 What does the word "challenging" (line 28) mean?

　　A Hazardous
　　B Stimulating
　　C Demanding
　　D Impossible

15 The author says that cycling can be "a way of life" (line 13). What does this mean?

　　A For some people, cycling is a job.
　　B Some people cycle to work or school.
　　C Some people can't live without cycling.
　　D Cycling affects how some people live their lives.

16 What does the phrase "up for grabs" (line 37) mean?

　　A Taken by force
　　B On display
　　C For everyone who competes
　　D To be won

Stop — you may check your answers in this section only

Section 2: Verbal Reasoning — Comprehension 2

 You have 8 minutes to complete this section

There are 10 questions in this section

Read the passage carefully and then answer the questions that follow.

The History of the Hollywood Sign

1   The Hollywood Sign is one of the most recognisable landmarks in the US. Throughout the history of cinema, images of the sign have permeated hundreds of movies, establishing a movie's setting in just one shot. The sight of the white letters, towering over the city below, immediately transports the audience to Los Angeles. Nowadays the sign and the movie
5   business are so inextricably linked that it is almost impossible to think of one without the other.

   However, this wasn't always the case. The sign originally read 'Hollywoodland', and it was erected by a local businessman named Harry Chandler. The sign was rigged with over 4000 light bulbs so it could be read at night. Chandler had intended that the sign would be in place for about 18 months, or as long as it took for him to fill the expensive housing estate
10 he was building. However, the sign proved so popular that Chandler never took it down. Thanks to the 'Golden Age of Hollywood' in the 1920s, the sign soon came to symbolise the flourishing movie industry that developed in the region.

   Because Chandler had not meant the sign to last, it was not made of the most resilient materials. There was no financial motivation for Chandler to maintain the sign, so it slowly
15 deteriorated. In the late 1940s, ownership of the sign was handed over to the city. The Great Depression meant that local residents weren't prepared to pay for the sign's maintenance, and it had become such an eyesore that most of them just wanted to be rid of it (the letter 'H' had been missing after being accidentally knocked over by the sign's caretaker in the early 1940s).

   In 1949 the Hollywood Chamber of Commerce agreed a deal with the City of Los Angeles
20 to take responsibility for the sign. Although they removed the light bulbs and the word 'land' from the sign, the maintenance costs continued to escalate, and the Chamber eventually found themselves unable to afford much-needed repairs. By the 1970s the sign was in its worst ever state: some letters had fallen over, others had rotted through. Anyone looking at the hillside in this period would have read the sign as 'HuLLYWO D'.

25 Fortunately, in 1978, a huge celebrity fund-raiser was organised to save the sign. Wealthy patrons agreed to pay for the sign to be rebuilt at a cost of more than $250 000. They invested in stronger materials so the new sign would last much longer than the old wooden letters. Construction began in August and the hillside was left without a sign for three months.

   These days the sign is looked after by the Hollywood Sign Trust. Even though the new
30 steel letters don't require much maintenance, the Trust still has to organise periodic repaints — no easy job, considering that each letter is 45 foot tall and between 31 and 40 feet wide. The Trust is also responsible for the sign's security, as well as arranging events to promote the sign (in 2013, for example, they celebrated the sign's 90th birthday with a huge party).

Answer these questions about the text. You can refer back to the text if you need to.
Pick the best answer and draw a line through the rectangle next to it.

1 Why was the sign first erected?

- A   It was meant to be a tourist attraction.
- B   Harry Chandler wanted to show how wealthy he was.
- C   It was meant to represent the movie business.
- D   It was part of an advertising campaign.

2 What would the sign probably have been read as in 1948?

- A   HOLLYWOODLAND
- B   OLLYWOOD
- C   HuLLYWO D
- D   OLLYWOODLAND

3 Which of these statements cannot be true?

- A   Chandler only intended the sign to be in place for a year and a half.
- B   The sign has always been painted white.
- C   The Hollywood Sign Trust was formed in 1978.
- D   The current sign is more than 400 feet wide.

4 For how long did the sign exist before the word 'land' was removed?

- A   Less than 10 years
- B   Exactly 20 years
- C   Around 25 years
- D   More than 40 years

5 Which of these statements must be true?

- A   All the local residents thought that the sign was an eyesore in the 1940s.
- B   In the original sign, each letter was around 45 foot tall.
- C   It cost less than $300 000 to replace the sign in 1978.
- D   There was a new sign in place by the start of 1979.

Go to the next question

6 Why did it cost so much to rebuild the sign in 1978?

- A Because it took a very long time to complete.
- B Because it was made from expensive materials.
- C Because the celebrities raised more money than was needed.
- D Because there were a lot of repairs to make.

7 Who owned the sign in 1938?

- A The Hollywood Sign Trust
- B The City of Los Angeles
- C Harry Chandler
- D The Hollywood Chamber of Commerce

8 Why do you think the Hollywood Chamber of Commerce removed the light bulbs?

- A Because they didn't work anymore.
- B Because the sign didn't need to be read at night any more.
- C Because it would have been expensive to replace them.
- D Because they thought it was tacky.

9 Why do you think the 1920s were known as the 'Golden Age of Hollywood'?

- A Because movies made in the 1920s had a yellow colour.
- B Because films were very expensive to make in the 1920s.
- C Because most actors and directors were paid in gold.
- D Because it was an extremely productive time for the movie business.

10 Why was the sign in a poor state of repair by 1940?

- A Because the caretaker had knocked over one of the letters.
- B Because the sign wasn't built to be weather resistant.
- C Because no one could afford to pay for the sign's maintenance.
- D Because some of the letters had rotted through.

 Stop — you may check your answers in this section only

Section 3: Verbal Reasoning — Multiple Meanings

Example Read this example question. You may return to this example at any time as you work through this section.

Choose the word which has a similar meaning to the words in both sets of brackets.

A (find discover) (stain blemish) freckle smudge **spot** see

Wait until you are told to go on

You have 4 minutes to complete this section

There are 12 questions in this section

Choose the word which has a similar meaning to the words in both sets of brackets.

1. (safe treasury) (shore beach) store bank bay secure
2. (encourage assist) (rear behind) back endorse tail end
3. (container canister) (clash irritate) ability jar bottle can
4. (alteration adjustment) (coins pennies) money adapt change excess
5. (understandable apparent) (absolve acquit) obvious free release clear
6. (impartial unprejudiced) (pale blond) fair just light honourable
7. (grip hold) (buy procure) tight grasp purchase trade
8. (betrothed committed) (occupied busy) full matched bound engaged
9. (shrub bush) (works factory) garden plant mill yard
10. (amusing trifling) (bright luminous) light shiny upbeat chirpy
11. (opposite reverse) (chat talk) confer converse contrary gossip
12. (licence warrant) (accept allow) charter pass authorise permit

Stop — you may check your answers in this section only

Section 4: Verbal Reasoning — Antonyms

Example Read this example question. You may return to this example at any time as you work through this section.

Complete the word on the right so that it means the opposite, or nearly the opposite, of the word on the left.

A strong   w e a k

⚠ **Wait until you are told to go on** ⚠

🕕 **You have 6 minutes to complete this section** 🕕

There are 16 questions in this section

Complete the word on the right so that it means the opposite, or nearly the opposite, of the word on the left.

1 important   t ☐ i ☐ ☐ a l

2 careless   c ☐ ☐ t i o ☐ s

3 unsophisticated   w ☐ ☐ l ☐ l y

4 sensible   f ☐ i ☐ ☐ l o u s

5 tough   f ☐ a ☐ l

6 friend   ☐ ☐ e

7) theoretical — p r _ v _ n
8) shallow — p _ o f o _ _ d
9) fixed — m _ b i _ _
10) uniform — _ a _ i _ d
11) conventional — q u _ r _ _
12) respectful — f l _ _ p _ n t
13) dynamic — p _ s _ i _ e
14) easy — _ r _ u o _ s
15) hurry — l _ _ t _ r
16) award — _ o _ f _ i t

Section 5: Verbal Reasoning — Synonyms

Example Read this example question. You may return to this example at any time as you work through this section.

Choose the word which means the same, or nearly the same, as the word on the left.

A small   tiny   strong   large   soft
              ■   ☐   ☐   ☐

⚠ **Wait until you are told to go on** ⚠

⏱ **You have 6 minutes to complete this section** ⏱

There are 18 questions in this section

Choose the word which means the same, or nearly the same, as the word on the left.

1. loathe   decline   renounce   despise   revere
              ☐   ☐   ☐   ☐

2. bare   dark   blighted   austere   gaunt
              ☐   ☐   ☐   ☐

3. encouraging   promising   interesting   impossible   selective
                 ☐   ☐   ☐   ☐

4. dazed   excited   blinded   gleeful   bewildered
              ☐   ☐   ☐   ☐

5. plenty   generous   full   abundance   deficit
              ☐   ☐   ☐   ☐

6. manic   enthusiastic   disturbed   delirious   berserk
              ☐   ☐   ☐   ☐

7. gaudy   rare   expensive   flamboyant   decorative
              ☐   ☐   ☐   ☐

8. random   irrelevant   casual   lucky   arbitrary
              ☐   ☐   ☐   ☐

#	Word	Options
9	**gloomy**	atmospheric ☐ monotonous ☐ ambient ☐ dismal ☐
10	**chirpy**	morose ☐ melodic ☐ cheerful ☐ energetic ☐
11	**cold**	frigid ☐ shiver ☐ passive ☐ temperate ☐
12	**amusing**	absurd ☐ droll ☐ clown ☐ quizzical ☐
13	**unsociable**	gregarious ☐ abrupt ☐ introverted ☐ restrained ☐
14	**glowing**	radiant ☐ pallid ☐ opaque ☐ blazing ☐
15	**compact**	crowded ☐ condensed ☐ foldable ☐ useful ☐
16	**creative**	talented ☐ artist ☐ inventive ☐ prolific ☐
17	**uninterested**	enthusiastic ☐ idle ☐ apathetic ☐ stolid ☐
18	**blocked**	congested ☐ busy ☐ crowded ☐ obstruction ☐

 Stop — you may check your answers in this section only

Section 6: Numerical Reasoning

Example Read these example questions. You may return to these examples at any time as you work through this section.

(A) Which of the following fractions is equivalent to ⁶⁄₈?   ¾ ▪   ½ ☐   ¹⁰⁄₁₆ ☐   ¹⁸⁄₃₆ ☐   ⅕ ☐

(B) Nassima bought 6 footballs. Each football cost £2.99. How much did she spend in total?   £ 1 7 . 9 4

⚠ **Wait until you are told to go on** ⚠

⏱ You have **9** minutes to complete this section ⏱

There are **23** questions in this section

(1) This mileometer shows how many miles a car has been driven.

099999

If Kyle drives the car one more mile, what will the new mileometer reading be?

☐☐☐☐☐☐ miles

(2) Tara starts at a number and counts on in steps of 7.
She counts to 31.
Which number could she have started from?

2 5 7 10 16
☐ ☐ ☐ ☐ ☐

(3) Round 7.038 to the nearest hundredth.   ☐.☐☐

(4) How many lines of symmetry does a regular octagon have?   ☐☐

5) Which of these shapes are prisms?

P   Q   R   S   T

- P, Q and S
- Q, R and T
- P and S only
- R and T only
- Only S

6) A dance club needed new shoes. They ordered the following sizes:

3   4   6   7   5   4   6   3   6   2

Which shoe size did they order the most of?

7) Which estimate best describes the height of an average car?

- 13 m
- 1.3 km
- 130 cm
- 130 mm
- 13 cm

8) The pictogram shows the number of cars of different colours in a car park.

Colour of car	Number of cars
silver	⦿ ⦿ ⦿ ⦿ ⦿
red	⦿ ⦿ ◖
black	⦿ ⦿ ◖
blue	⦿ ⦿ ⦿ ⦿ ◖
green	⦿ ◖

⦿ = 4 cars

How many more silver cars were there than black cars in the car park?

9) There are 24 people on a bus.
8 people get off the bus and 5 people get on.
How many people are on the bus now?

10) A number is exactly divisible by 3 and 4.
Which of these numbers could it be?

- 210
- 330
- 340
- 400
- 480

(11) What is the size of the missing angle x in this triangle?

100°, 27°

☐☐☐ °

(12) Claire is sharing a cake between her friends. She cuts it into 24 pieces and gives 18 away. What fraction of the cake does she have left?

3/4 ☐   1/3 ☐   1/4 ☐   2/9 ☐   4/9 ☐

(13) Leila buys 137 boxes of pencils for her school. Each box contains 44 pencils. In total she has 6028 pencils. She also orders 137 boxes of erasers. Each box contains 22 erasers. How many erasers does Leila have in total?

☐☐☐☐

(14) If the 4th of June is a Monday, what day of the week is the 27th of June?

Monday ☐   Tuesday ☐   Wednesday ☐   Thursday ☐   Friday ☐

(15) This machine divides a number by 3 and then adds 8.

? → ÷3 → +8 → 32

What number was put into the machine?

☐☐☐

(16) A supermarket checks the temperature of its storeroom. At 10 am the temperature was −6 °C. By 10 pm it had fallen by 9 °C. What was the temperature of the storeroom at 10 pm?

−☐☐ °C

(17) Kai buys a book for £4.99 and a birthday card for £1.45. What change does he get from £10?

£☐.☐☐

18 In Amina's school there are 560 children.
45% of the children have blue as their favourite colour.
How many children in the school like blue the best?

19 What are the coordinates of point B on the hexagon to the right?

20 Andrew has £21.60 and Julie has £15.40. Andrew wants to give some of his money to Julie so that they have an equal amount. How much money does Andrew need to give Julie?

£ ☐☐.☐☐

21 Pradip has £15 in his savings. He plans to save £2 each week.
Which expression shows how much money in pounds he will have after n weeks?

$15n$ $2n$ $2n + 15n$ $2n + 15$ $17n$

22 Jay has morning lessons from 8.40 am until lunch at midday.
He stops for a morning break that lasts from 10.35 am until 10.50 am.
How long does Jay spend in morning lessons?

☐ hours ☐☐ minutes

23 Chocolates can have hard centres or soft centres.
A box of chocolates has twice as many hard-centred chocolates as soft-centred ones. There are 22 soft-centred chocolates in the box. How many chocolates are there in the box in total?

Stop — you may check your answers in this section only

BLANK PAGE

11+ Practice Paper

For Ages 10-11

Set A: Paper 2
For the CEM Test

Read the following:

Do not open this booklet or start the test until you are told to do so.

1. This test can be taken in either multiple-choice or write-in format.

2. If you are taking it as a multiple-choice test, you should mark your answer to each question in pencil on the separate answer sheet. Mark the correct box quickly and neatly using a horizontal line.

3. If you are taking it as a write-in test, you should write your answer to each question in pencil on the paper. Write your answer carefully in the space provided or, if there is a range of options, mark the correct box quickly and neatly using a horizontal line.

4. If you make a mistake, rub it out and mark your new answer clearly.

5. There are three sections in this test.

6. The time allowed for each section is given at the start of that section. You will have a total of 45 minutes to complete the timed sections of the test.

7. Each section includes examples showing you how to answer the questions. You may refer to these examples at any time as you work through the section.

8. Do as many questions as you can. For some questions you will be given a range of options — if you get stuck on one of these questions, choose the answer that you think is most likely to be correct, then move on to the next question. If you get stuck on a question for which no options are given, leave it and move on to the next question. If you have time at the end of the section, go back and have another go at the questions you could not answer.

9. You should do any rough working on a separate piece of paper.

Work carefully, but go as quickly as you can.

Section 1: Verbal Reasoning — Cloze

Example Read these example questions. You may return to these examples at any time as you work through this section.

Tea is often thought of as a traditional English drink. (A) ☐ Despite / ■ However / ☐ Also / ☐ While, it was popular in

China centuries before it (B) ☐ brought / ☐ drunk / ☐ travelled / ■ arrived in Europe.

⚠ Wait until you are told to go on ⚠

You have 6 minutes to complete this section

There are 16 questions in this section

Giant pandas are the (1) ☐ rare / ☐ rarest / ☐ rarer / ☐ rarely bear species on the planet.

They are (2) ☐ exposed / ☐ original / ☐ related / ☐ native to China where they are (3) ☐ considered / ☐ admired / ☐ resolved / ☐ granted to be a

national treasure and are often used to (4) ☐ misrepresent / ☐ define / ☐ symbolise / ☐ operate the country.

Their distinctive black and white markings and (5) ☐ reputation / ☐ greed / ☐ ability / ☐ diet for eating vast

amounts of bamboo mean that they are (6) ☐ experienced / ☐ recognised / ☐ understood / ☐ replicated all over the world.

Giant pandas may look (7) ☐ about / ☐ like / ☐ for / ☐ of massive teddy bears, but their

(8)
- appearance
- size
- strength
- charm

should not be underestimated. Giant pandas have been known to attack humans,

(9)
- although
- sometimes
- therefore
- possibly

rarely without provocation.

Due to human activity (mainly the

(10)
- conservation
- planting
- growth
- destruction

of the bamboo forests where they live), they are an endangered species, and

(11)
- some
- only
- almost
- over

1 600 were

(12)
- records
- recorded
- record
- recording

as living in the wild in 2004.

Giant pandas play an essential

(13)
- game
- job
- role
- position

in the forests where they reside.

They

(14)
- disperse
- plant
- gather
- arrange

seeds in their waste as they roam through the trees, so without these bears, the

(15)
- climate
- growth
- knowledge
- colour

of the forest would suffer.

Conservation and breeding projects have been established around the world in an attempt to

(16)
- preserve
- diminish
- prevent
- savour

the giant panda and its habitat.

Stop — you may check your answers in this section only

Section 2: Numerical Reasoning

Example Read these example questions. You may return to these examples at any time as you work through this section.

A George draws a graph showing a flight by his remote-control model plane.

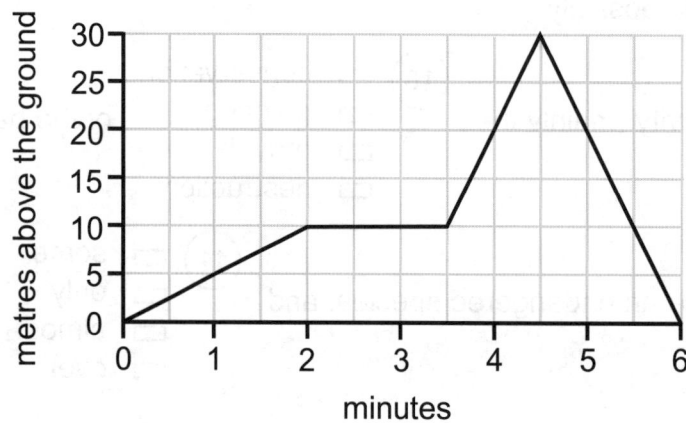

A1 How long did the flight last? [6] minutes

A2 How high was the plane after 4 minutes of flight? [2][0] m

A3 According to the graph, what was the plane doing between 3½ and 4½ minutes of flight?

speeding up ☐ rising ▭ slowing down ☐ falling ☐

Wait until you are told to go on

You have 25 minutes to complete this section

There are **9** multi-part questions in this section

1 Here is a diagram of Basma's back garden.

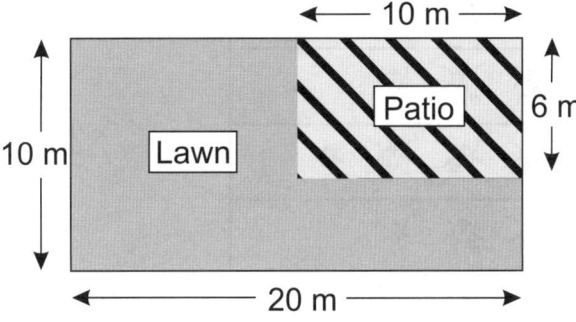

a) What is the area of Basma's lawn? ☐☐☐ m²

b) Basma digs up 20 m² of her lawn to make a flower bed.
What fraction is this of Basma's lawn?

$\frac{1}{14}$ $\frac{1}{10}$ $\frac{2}{7}$ $\frac{1}{7}$ $\frac{3}{14}$
☐ ☐ ☐ ☐ ☐

c) Basma then decides she wants to cover 20% of the remaining lawn with decking.
How many m² is this? ☐☐☐ m²

Go to the next question →

2) Robbie counted the number of ladybirds in his garden over a week.
He made a pictogram of his results.

Monday	🐞🐞🐞🐞🐞🐞🐞
Tuesday	🐞🐞🐞
Wednesday	🐞🐞🐞🐞
Thursday	🐞🐞🐞🐞
Friday	🐞🐞🐞🐞
Saturday	🐞🐞🐞
Sunday	🐞🐞

 = 4 ladybirds

a) How many more ladybirds did Robbie see in total on Wednesday and Thursday than on Saturday and Sunday?

b) What is the most common number of ladybirds that Robbie counted on any one day over the week?

c) What is the mean number of ladybirds that Robbie counted on any one day over the week?

3) This chart shows the distances in kilometres between six cities in France.

Calais					
574	Dijon				
111	504	Lille			
1258	684	1188	Nice		
294	312	224	952	Paris	
534	416	464	928	237	Tours

a) Isabelle travels exactly 224 kilometres. Between which two cities did she travel?

Calais and Paris ☐   Paris and Dijon ☐   Nice and Lille ☐   Lille and Paris ☐   Tours and Lille ☐

b) Hasim travels from Lille to Tours.
Mary travels from Lille to Calais.
How much further does Hasim travel than Mary?   ☐☐☐☐ km

c) Juliette starts on a journey from Dijon to Lille.
She travels ¾ of the distance in the first day before stopping for the night.
She travels the remainder of the distance the next day.
How far does she travel on the second day?   ☐☐☐☐ km

d) Marco needs to drive from Nice to Calais.
His car can drive 250 kilometres on a full tank of petrol.
Marco starts in Nice with a full tank of petrol.
What is the fewest number of times Marco can stop to fill up his car on his way to Calais?   ☐☐

Go to the next question

4) Two friends, Karim and Dave, each have a savings account at the bank. They pay money into their accounts each month. The tables below show the total amounts in their accounts at the end of each month.

Month	Amount in account (£)
1	2
2	4
3	8
4	16
5	32
6	?

Karim

Month	Amount in account (£)
1	14
2	38
3	62
4	86
5	110
6	134

Dave

a) If Karim continues to save his money following the same pattern, how much will he have saved by the end of the 6th month?

£ ☐☐☐

b) Which expression describes the amount that Dave has in his account at the end of each month, m?

$m + 14$ ☐ $200m - 6$ ☐ $14m + 10$ ☐ $24m - 10$ ☐ $24m \div 2$ ☐

c) Who will have saved the most money by the end of the 8th month?

Dave ☐   Karim ☐   Both equal ☐

5) This pie chart shows the percentage of flowering plants bought from a garden centre.

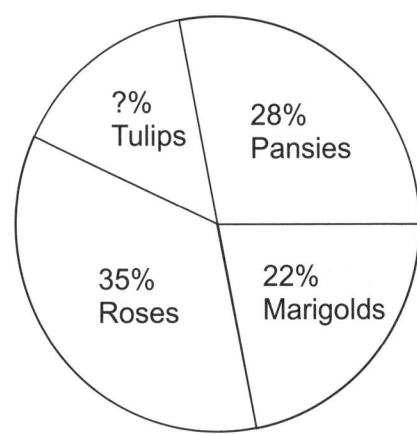

a) Altogether, 500 plants were sold. How many tulips were sold?

b) Red and white roses were sold at a ratio of 4:1. How many red roses were sold?

The prices of the different flowering plants at the garden centre are in the table below.

Plant	Price (£)
Tulips	£7.50
Red Roses	£12
White Roses	£11.50
Marigolds	£9
Pansies	£4.50

c) What was the total value of all the pansies sold by the garden centre?

£

Go to the next question

6 Below are the timetables of events and tours for a day at Whitterby Zoo. The zoo is open from 9:30 until 17:30.

There are no pauses in between events.

Time	Event
10:00	Penguin Feeding
10:30	African Adventure
12:10	Big Cat Talk
12:45	Lunch with Lions
13:50	Gorilla Feeding
14:15	Sea Lion Display
15:00	Monkey Tricks
15:40	Zebra Feeding
16:00	Camel Rides
16:55	Talking with Parrots

Zoo Tours	
Morning: 9:30 - 11:45	Every 15 minutes. Duration: 10 minutes.
Lunch: 11:55 - 1:30	There will be no tours over the lunch break.
Afternoon: 1:30 - 5:15	Every 20 minutes. Duration: 15 minutes

a) Which of these events is the shortest?

Penguin Feeding ☐   Big Cat Talk ☐   Gorilla Feeding ☐   Zebra Feeding ☐   Camel Rides ☐

b) How much longer is the African Adventure than the Gorilla Feeding?

☐☐☐ minutes

c) Jane arrives at the zoo at 12:10. She goes on the first tour she can after she arrives. What event is happening when she finishes the tour?

Big Cat Talk ☐   Lunch with Lions ☐   Gorilla Feeding ☐   Sea Lion Display ☐   Monkey Tricks ☐

d) Ramla goes to the Big Cat Talk. After it finishes she wants to go on a tour. How long will she have to wait before a tour starts?

☐☐☐ minutes

7 Jimmie has a puzzle which is the shape of a regular hexagon.
The puzzle has 6 identical pieces.

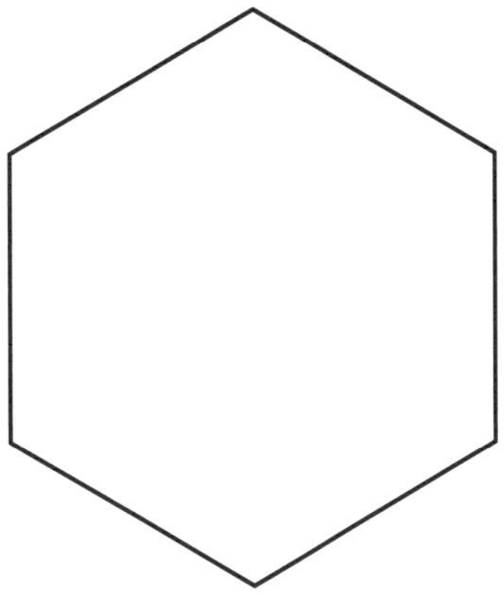

a) Which of the following pieces would fit inside the puzzle 6 times with no overlap and cover the full space?

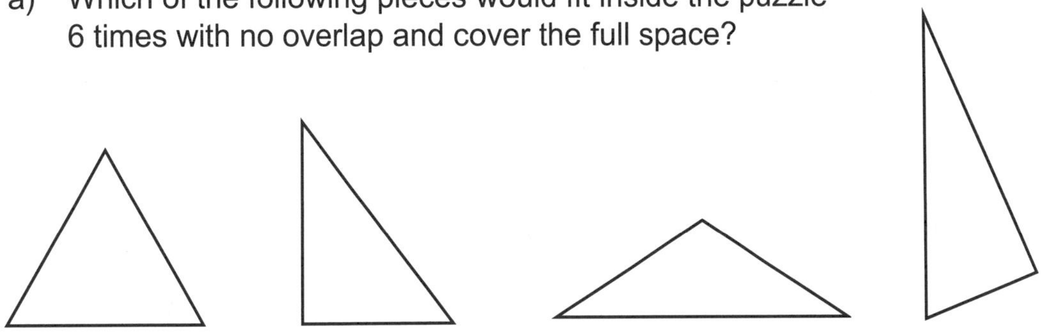

A ☐   B ☐   C ☐   D ☐

b) How many lines of symmetry does the puzzle have?

c) Jimmie has two identical puzzle pieces, shown on the right, each shaped like a parallelogram. He is allowed to rotate and translate the pieces to make a combined shape.
Which of these shapes will he not be able to make?

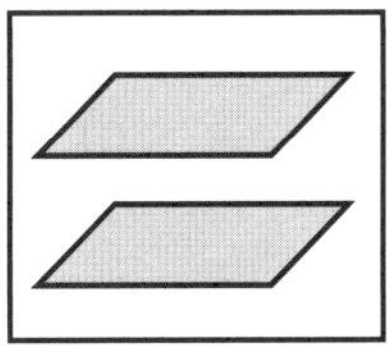

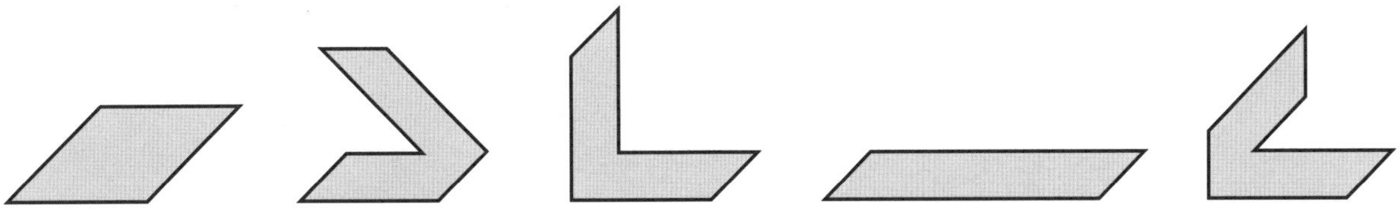

A ☐   B ☐   C ☐   D ☐   E ☐

Go to the next question

8) The map below shows a plan of Pranav's garden.
Each square corresponds to 1 metre.

a) What are the coordinates of the swings?

| (8, −2) | (1, 8) | (2, 8) | (−2, 8) | (−2, −8) |
| □ | □ | □ | □ | □ |

b) Pranav stands at the flower bed. He walks 2 metres east and 10 metres north. What point in the garden has Pranav reached?

| Tree House | Bird House | Fountain | Pond | Swings |
| □ | □ | □ | □ | □ |

c) Pranav stands at the swings. He walks 6 metres south and turns to face south west. What is Pranav looking at?

| Tree House | Lake | Flower Bed | Shed | Bird House |
| □ | □ | □ | □ | □ |

d) What is at the point that is equivalent to the reflection of the pond in the x-axis?

| Shed | Fountain | Flower Bed | Lake | Tree House |
| □ | □ | □ | □ | □ |

9 The graph shows the cost of sending parcels with two different companies.

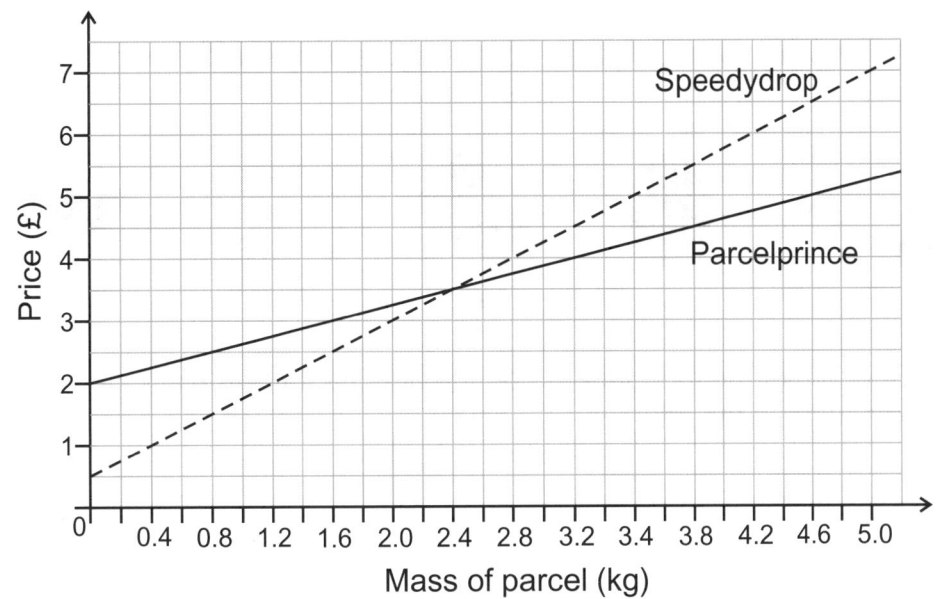

a) Sania is sending a present to a friend.
The present has a mass of 1.55 kg.
It is packed inside a box that has a mass of 0.05 kg.
What is the smallest amount that Sania can spend to send her parcel?

£ 2.24

b) Georgina packs 2 books into one parcel to be posted. The books have a mass of 2.2 kg and 1.6 kg, and the packaging has a mass of 0.8 kg. How much will Georgina pay if she uses the cheapest company?

£ 4.76

c) Harry needs to send two separate parcels. One has a mass of 0.8 kg and the other has a mass of 3.2 kg. He wants to use the same company to send both parcels. What is the smallest amount Harry will have to pay using the same company?

£ 5.60

Stop — you may check your answers in this section only

Section 3: Non-Verbal Reasoning

Example Read these example questions. You may return to these examples at any time as you work through this section.

A Work out which option would look like the figure on the left if it was rotated:

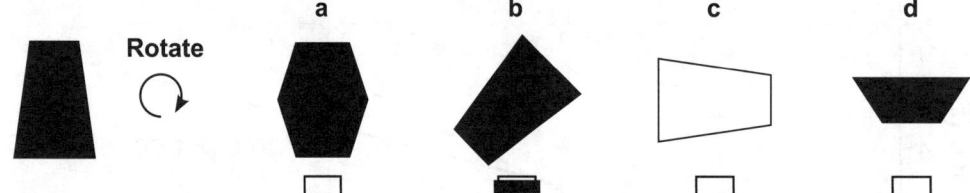

B Work out which of the four squares on the right best fits in place of the missing square in the grid:

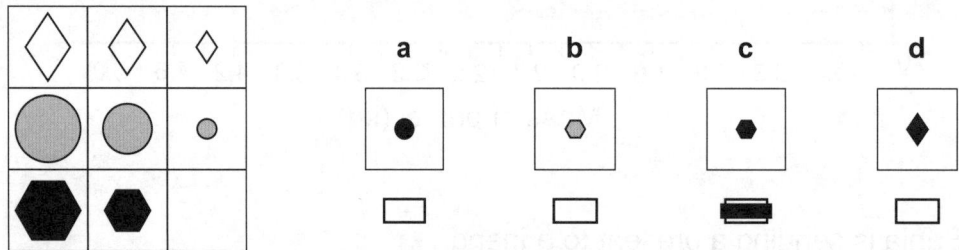

C Find the figure in each row that is most unlike the other figures:

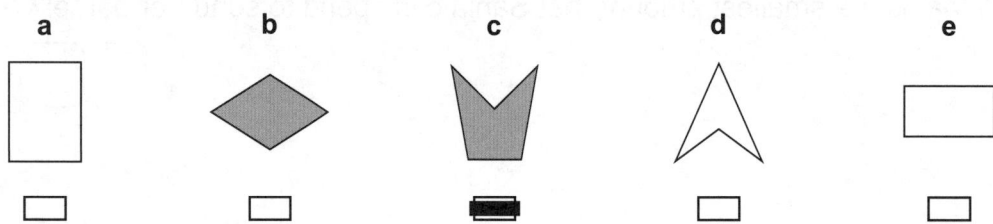

D Work out which of the four squares on the right best fits in place of the missing square in the series:

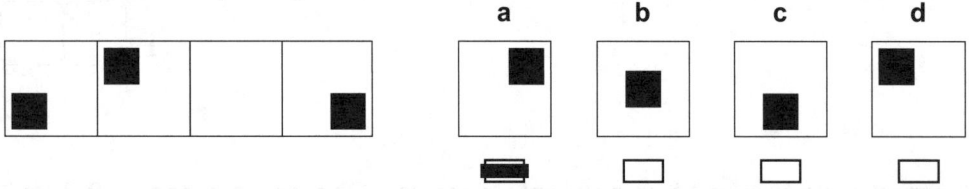

E Work out which option would look like the figure on the left if it was reflected over the vertical line:

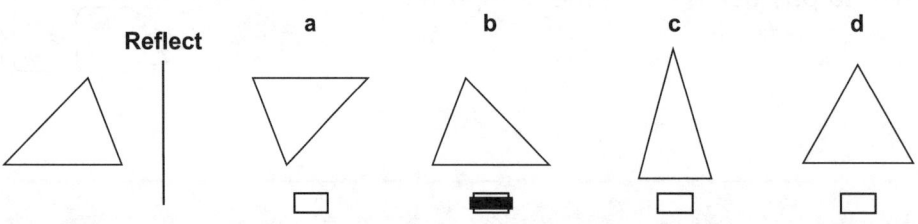

Wait until you are told to go on

You have 14 minutes to complete this section

There are 34 questions in this section

Work out which option would look like the figure on the left if it was rotated:

1      a    b 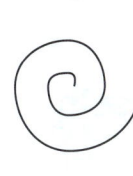   c    d

2      a    b    c 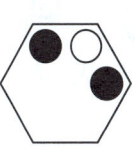   d

3      a    b    c    d

4   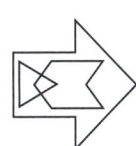    a    b    c    d

5      a   b    c 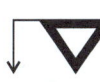   d

Go to the next question

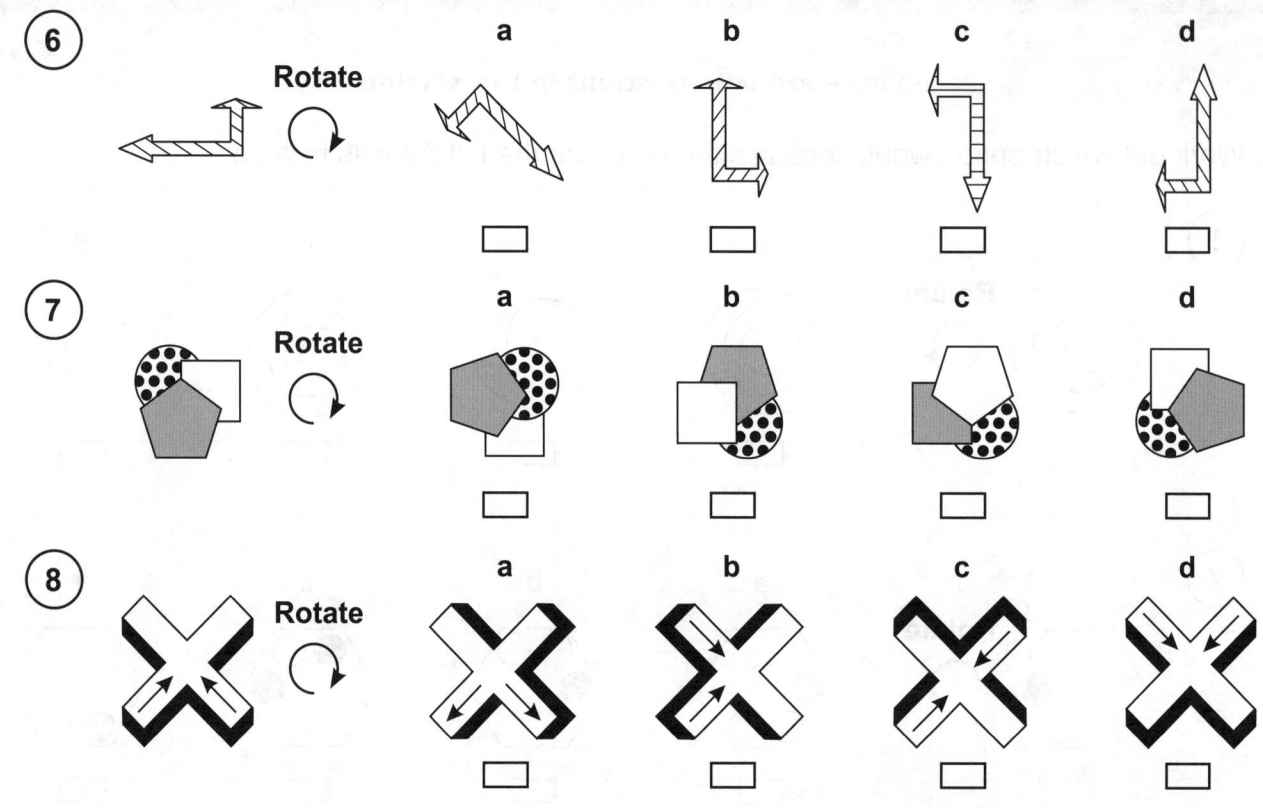

Work out which of the four squares on the right best fits in place of the missing square in the grid:

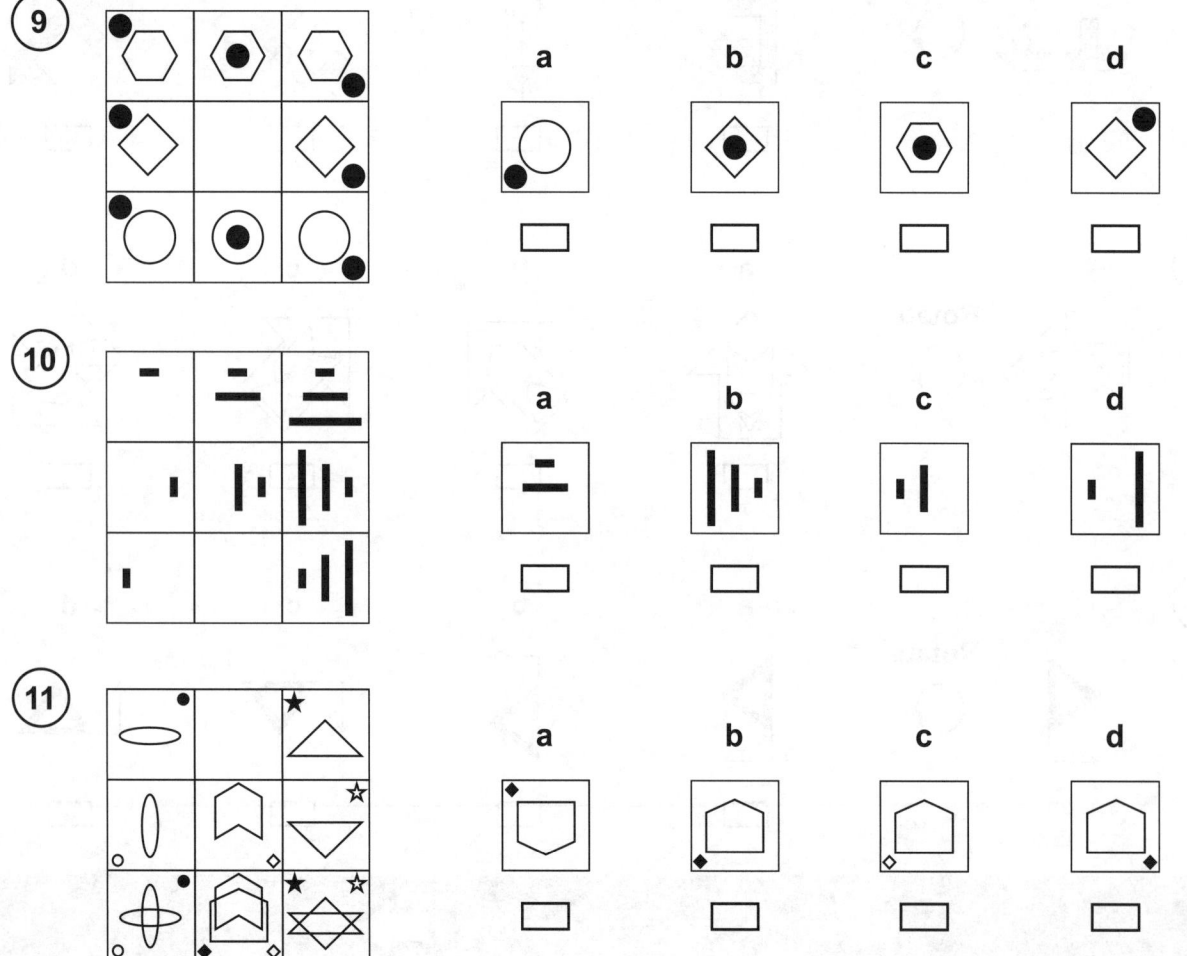

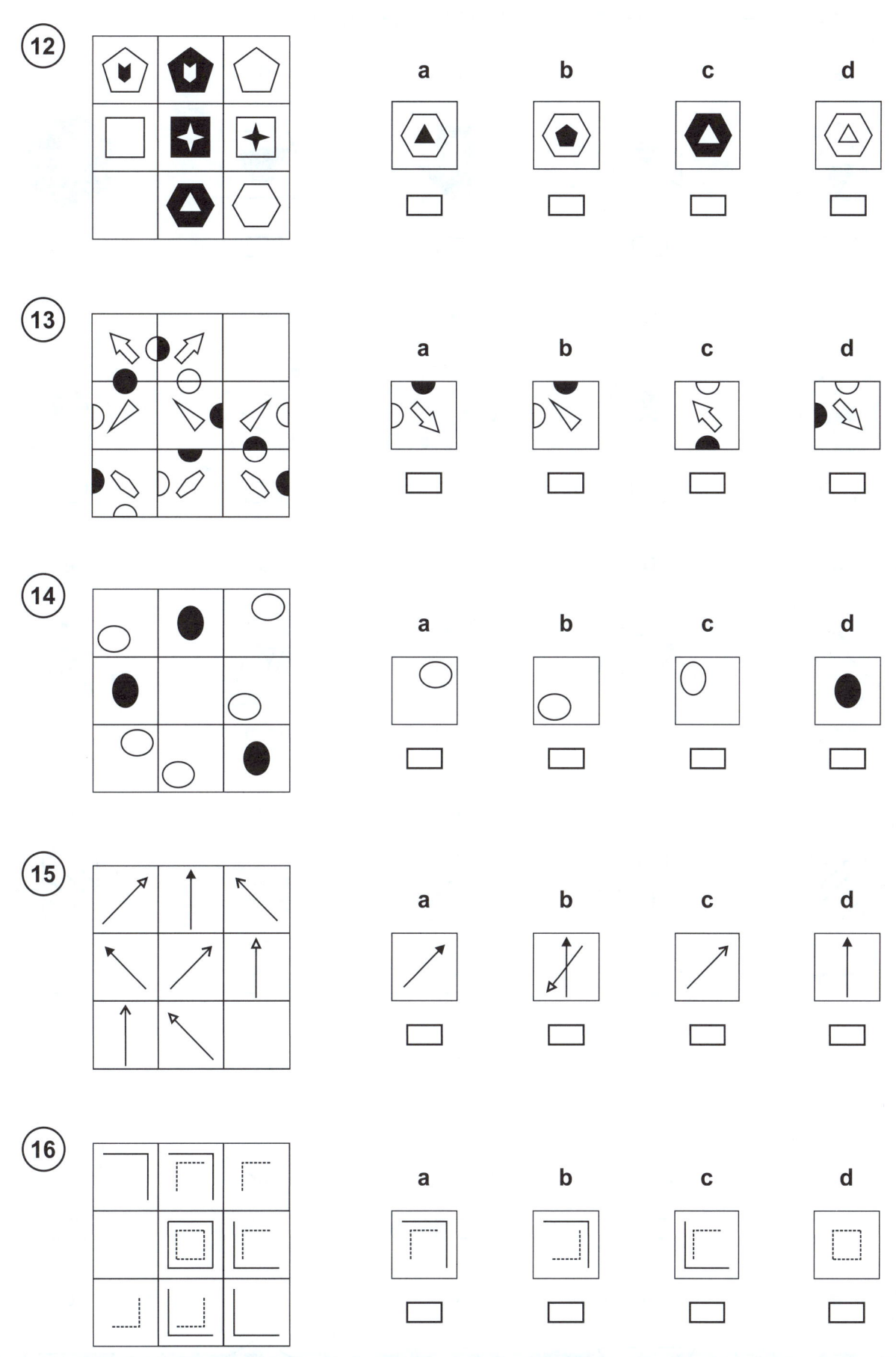

Find the figure in each row that is most unlike the other figures:

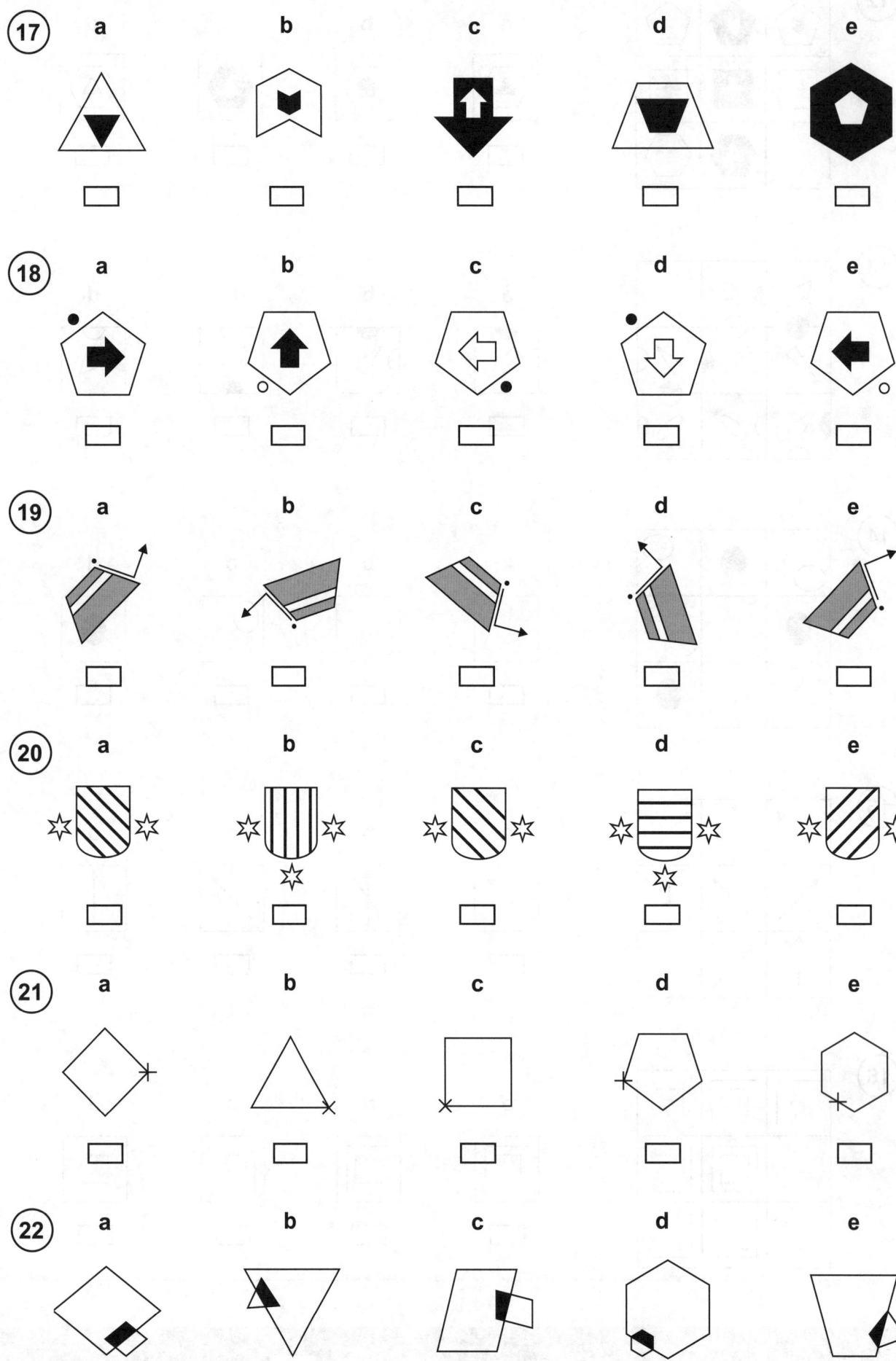

Work out which of the four squares on the right best fits in place of the missing square in the series:

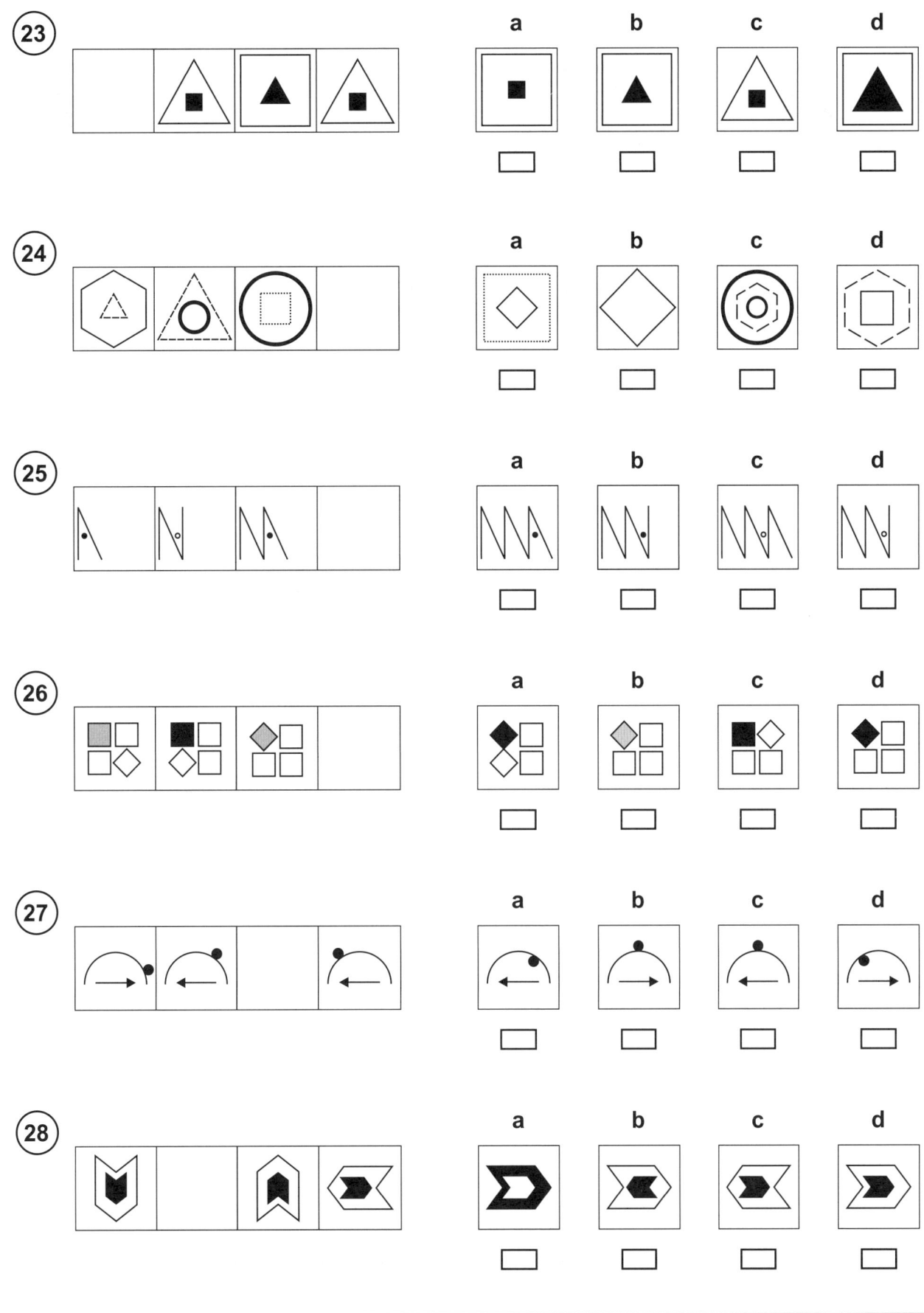

Work out which option would look like the figure on the left if it was reflected over the vertical line:

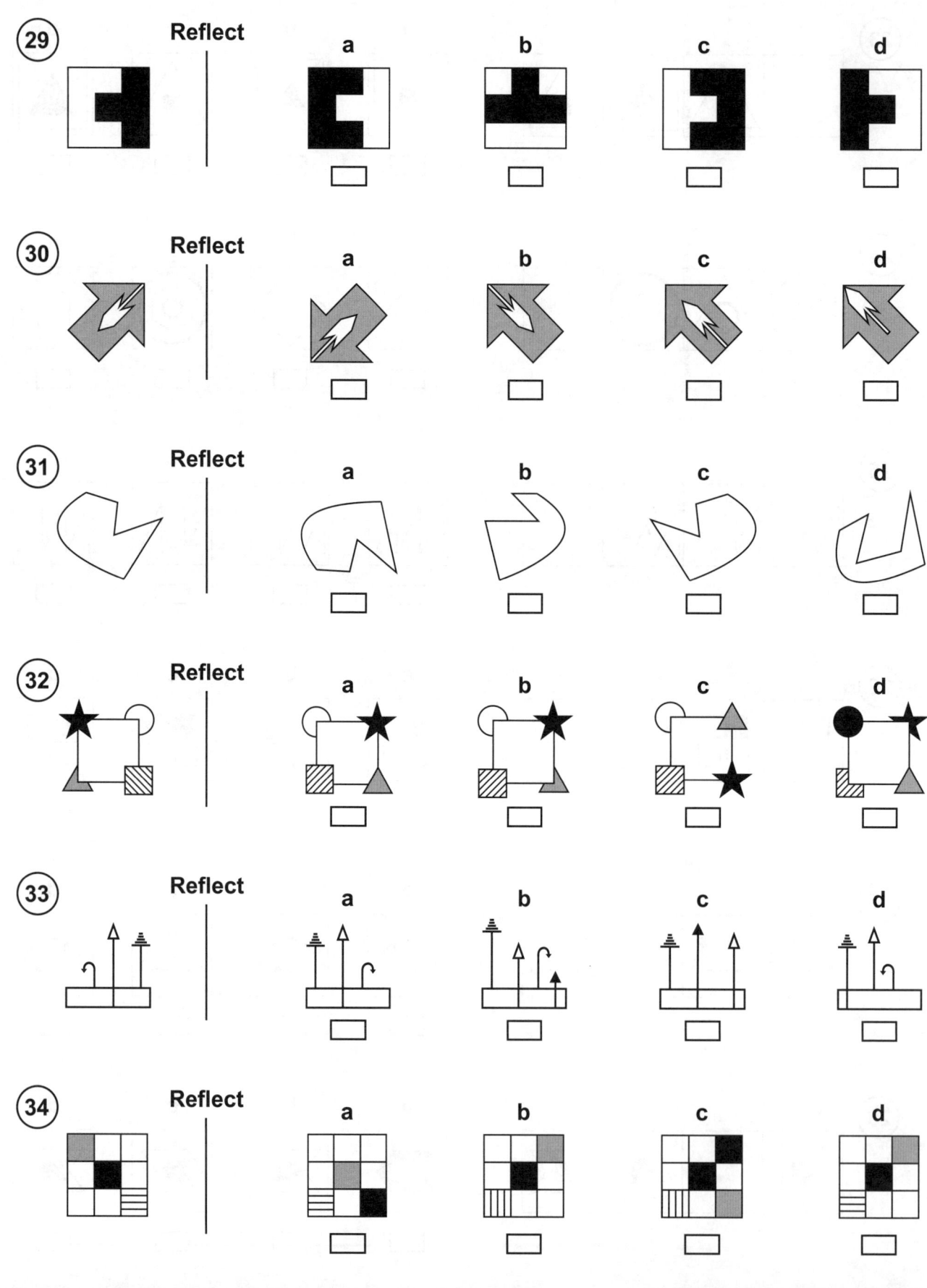

11+ Practice Paper

For Ages 10-11

Set B: Paper 1
For the CEM Test

Read the following:

Do not open this booklet or start the test until you are told to do so.

1. This test can be taken in either multiple-choice or write-in format.

2. If you are taking it as a multiple-choice test, you should mark your answer to each question in pencil on the separate answer sheet. Mark the correct box quickly and neatly using a horizontal line.

3. If you are taking it as a write-in test, you should write your answer to each question in pencil on the paper. Write your answer carefully in the space provided or, if there is a range of options, mark the correct box quickly and neatly using a horizontal line.

4. If you make a mistake, rub it out and mark your new answer clearly.

5. There are five sections in this test.

6. The time allowed for each section is given at the start of that section. You will have a total of 45 minutes to complete the timed sections of the test.

7. Each section includes examples showing you how to answer the questions. You may refer to these examples at any time as you work through the section.

8. Do as many questions as you can. For some questions you will be given a range of options — if you get stuck on one of these questions, choose the answer that you think is most likely to be correct, then move on to the next question. If you get stuck on a question for which no options are given, leave it and move on to the next question. If you have time at the end of the section, go back and have another go at the questions you could not answer.

9. You should do any rough working on a separate piece of paper.

Work carefully, but go as quickly as you can.

Section 1: Verbal Reasoning — Comprehension

Example — Read these example questions. You may return to these examples at any time as you work through this section.

HMS Iolaire — A Tragedy Follows a Victory

1   World War I had just ended, the Armistice had been agreed, and a large number of sailors were making their way home to Stornoway on the island of Lewis, off the west coast of Scotland. They were looking forward to coming home.

   However, in the early hours of January 1st, 1919, disaster struck. HMS Iolaire
5   crashed into the notorious 'Beasts of Holm', a set of rocks just a mile away from the safety of Stornoway harbour. Around 50 men jumped overboard, planning to swim the short distance to the shore. Sadly, the stormy seas and windy conditions meant that these men perished. Meanwhile, there were many fatalities on board as the ship began to sink. The alarm was raised and the town's coastguard was called out, but by
10 the time he and his team arrived at the scene of the disaster, the ship had sunk.

A Why did the sailors have to travel to Stornoway by boat?

- ☐ A   Because Stornoway is on the west coast of Scotland
- ☐ B   Because they were on their way back from World War I
- ■ C   Because Stornoway is on an island
- ☐ D   Because the 'Beasts of Holm' were dangerous

B The 'Beasts of Holm' are described as "notorious" (line 5). What is meant by this?

- ☐ A   The rocks were concealed from view.
- ■ B   The rocks were well known for being dangerous.
- ☐ C   Many people admired the rocks.
- ☐ D   The rocks had a mysterious reputation.

End of example questions

 Wait until you are told to go on

You have 15 minutes to complete this section

There are 20 questions in this section

Read the passage carefully and then answer the questions that follow.

An extract from 'Oliver Twist'

1   Oliver reached the stile at which the by-path terminated; and once more gained the high-road. It was eight o'clock now. Though he was nearly five miles away from the town, he ran, and hid behind the hedges, by turns, till noon: fearing that he might be pursued and overtaken. Then he sat down to rest by the side of the milestone, and began to think, for the
5   first time, where he had better go and try to live.

The stone by which he was seated, bore, in large characters, an intimation that it was just seventy miles from that spot to London. The name awakened a new train of ideas in the boy's mind.

London! — that great place! — nobody — not even Mr. Bumble — could ever find him there!
10   He had often heard the old men in the workhouse, too, say that no lad of spirit need want in London; and that there were ways of living in that vast city, which those who had been bred up in country parts had no idea of. It was the very place for a homeless boy, who must die in the streets unless some one helped him. As these things passed through his thoughts, he jumped upon his feet, and again walked forward.

15   He had diminished the distance between himself and London by full four miles more, before he recollected how much he must undergo ere* he could hope to reach his place of destination. As this consideration forced itself upon him, he slackened his pace a little, and meditated upon his means of getting there. He had a crust of bread, a coarse shirt, and two pairs of stockings, in his bundle. He had a penny too — a gift of Sowerberry's after some
20   funeral in which he had acquitted himself more than ordinarily well — in his pocket. 'A clean shirt,' thought Oliver, 'is a very comfortable thing; and so are two pairs of darned stockings; and so is a penny; but they are small helps to a sixty-five miles' walk in winter time.' But Oliver's thoughts, like those of most other people, although they were extremely ready and active to point out his difficulties, were wholly at a loss to suggest any feasible mode of
25   surmounting them; so, after a good deal of thinking to no particular purpose, he changed his little bundle over to the other shoulder, and trudged on.

Oliver walked twenty miles that day; and all that time tasted nothing but the crust of dry bread, and a few draughts of water, which he begged at the cottage-doors by the road-side. When the night came, he turned into a meadow; and, creeping close under a hay-rick,
30   determined to lie there, till morning. He felt frightened at first, for the wind moaned dismally

Passage continues over the page

over the empty fields: and he was cold and hungry, and more alone than he had ever felt before. Being very tired with his walk, however, he soon fell asleep and forgot his troubles.

He felt cold and stiff, when he got up next morning, and so hungry that he was obliged to exchange the penny for a small loaf, in the very first village through which he passed. He had walked no more than twelve miles, when night closed in again. His feet were sore, and his legs so weak that they trembled beneath him. Another night passed in the bleak damp air, made him worse; when he set forward on his journey next morning he could hardly crawl along.

He waited at the bottom of a steep hill till a stage-coach came up, and then begged of the outside passengers; but there were very few who took any notice of him: and even those told him to wait till they got to the top of the hill, and then let them see how far he could run for a halfpenny. Poor Oliver tried to keep up with the coach a little way, but was unable to do it, by reason of his fatigue and sore feet. When the outsides saw this, they put their halfpence back into their pockets again, declaring that he was an idle young dog, and didn't deserve anything; and the coach rattled away and left only a cloud of dust behind.

In some villages, large painted boards were fixed up: warning all persons who begged within the district, that they would be sent to jail. This frightened Oliver very much, and made him glad to get out of those villages with all possible expedition. In others, he would stand about the inn-yards, and look mournfully at every one who passed: a proceeding which generally terminated in the landlady's ordering one of the post-boys who were lounging about, to drive that strange boy out of the place, for she was sure he had come to steal something. If he begged at a farmer's house, ten to one but they threatened to set the dog on him; and when he showed his nose in a shop, they talked about the beadle** — which brought Oliver's heart into his mouth, — very often the only thing he had there, for many hours together.

by Charles Dickens

* ere — before
** beadle — an official responsible for the workhouse and orphanage

Answer these questions about the text. You can refer back to the text if you need to.
Pick the best answer and draw a line through the rectangle next to it.

1 How do you know that Oliver is running away from someone at the start of the extract?

- A   He runs as fast as he can.
- B   He hasn't decided where he's going.
- C   He's afraid he's being followed.
- D   He left early in the morning.

2 How does Oliver feel when he realises that he is seventy miles away from London?

- A   Disheartened
- B   Content
- C   Re-energised
- D   Frightened

3 What is the main reason that Oliver decides to go to London?

- A   It's the capital city.
- B   It's very far away.
- C   The men in the workhouse told him to.
- D   Nobody will be able to find him there.

4 Which of these things does Oliver not have in his bundle?

- A   A penny
- B   A clean shirt
- C   A crust of bread
- D   A pair of stockings

5 The author says that Oliver did a "good deal of thinking to no particular purpose" (line 25). This tells us that:

- A   Oliver doesn't know how he will get to London.
- B   Oliver is too tired to think properly.
- C   Oliver isn't thinking of anything specific.
- D   Oliver doesn't know where he's going to go.

Go to the next question

6 Where did Oliver get his penny?

☐ A   He stole it from Sowerberry.
☐ B   Sowerberry left it to him in his will.
☐ C   He earned it by working for Sowerberry.
☐ D   He was given it at Sowerberry's funeral.

7 Why is Oliver "frightened at first" (line 30) after deciding to sleep under a hay-rick?

☐ A   He's not allowed to sleep there.
☐ B   The sound of the wind scares him.
☐ C   He thinks Mr Bumble might find him.
☐ D   His walk made him tired.

8 How far has Oliver walked in total by the end of the second day?

☐ A   Twenty miles
☐ B   Twelve miles
☐ C   Sixty-five miles
☐ D   Thirty-two miles

9 Why did the coach passengers call Oliver "an idle young dog" (line 44)?

☐ A   Because he ran too slowly.
☐ B   Because he crawled on his hands and knees.
☐ C   Because he's lazy.
☐ D   Because he didn't deserve any money.

10 Why is Oliver afraid he'll be sent to jail?

☐ A   Begging is illegal.
☐ B   It's illegal for children to be out on their own.
☐ C   Shopkeepers threaten to send for the beadle.
☐ D   He stole food from shops.

11 Which of these words best describes the landladies' attitude towards Oliver?

- A Suspicious
- B Bitter
- C Inquisitive
- D Uncertain

12 Which of these people help Oliver?

- A Post-boys
- B Shopkeepers
- C Passengers on the coach
- D People who live in cottages

13 Why does Oliver describe his possessions as "small helps" (line 22)?

- A He's used to having lots of belongings.
- B They are a handy size for travelling.
- C He doesn't think they'll be very useful.
- D He thinks they'll help him on his journey.

14 Why do you think Oliver "slackened his pace a little" (line 17)?

- A He's getting tired.
- B His bag is heavy.
- C He's realised how difficult the journey will be.
- D He's not sure which way to go.

15 How do you think Oliver feels as the stage-coach leaves?

- A Flustered
- B Exhausted
- C Relieved
- D Bewildered

Go to the next question

16 What does the word "diminished" (line 15) mean?

- A Reduced
- B Extended
- C Weakened
- D Calculated

17 What does the word "surmounting" (line 25) mean?

- A Increasing
- B Delaying
- C Overcoming
- D Improving

18 What does the word "obliged" (line 33) mean?

- A Grateful
- B Urged
- C Eager
- D Forced

19 What is meant by the phrase "awakened a new train of ideas" (line 7)?

- A Made him feel more enthusiastic.
- B Made him think of a new plan.
- C Made him think the journey would be easier.
- D Made him change his mind about his journey.

20 What is meant by the phrase "brought Oliver's heart into his mouth" (lines 53-54)?

- A Made Oliver even more hungry.
- B Made Oliver say how he really felt.
- C Made Oliver feel sick.
- D Made Oliver frightened.

Stop — you may check your answers in this section only

BLANK PAGE

Section 2: Verbal Reasoning — Cloze

Example Read these example questions. You may return to these examples at any time as you work through this section.

A. The Solar System is made up of [p][l][a][n][e][t][s], asteroids and other

B. bodies orbiting the Sun. Earth is the [t][h][i][r][d] planet from the Sun,

C. after Mercury and [V][e][n][u][s].

Wait until you are told to go on

You have 9 minutes to complete this section

There are 21 questions in this section

The Bermuda Triangle, or Devil's Triangle, is an area of the

1. [A][t][ ][ ][n][t][ ][ ] Ocean off the southeast coast of the United States.

2. There is no formal [ ][o][c][a][ ][ ][o][n] for the triangle, and it can't be found

3. on any [o][f][f][ ][ ][ ][ ][l] maps. However, many ships and aircraft

4. are [a][l][ ][e][g][ ][d] to have gone missing,

5. and numerous sailors have had [b][i][z][ ][ ][ ][e] experiences

6. in the triangle of ocean [ ][e][t][ ][e][ ][n] Miami, Puerto Rico and Bermuda.

7. Bermuda itself was once [k][ ][ ][ ][n] as the 'Isle of Devils' because large

8. areas of reefs which surround the island were a serious [t][ ][r][ ][ ][t] to boats

9. that sailed too close to its [s][ ][o][ ][s].

10. One of the most [p][ ][ ][ ][l][i][a][r] incidents in the history of the

11) Bermuda Triangle was the disappearance of five bomber p l _ _ _ s from

12) 'Flight 19' in 1945. A training flight of five aircraft left a n _ v _ l

base in Florida, but none of them returned.

13) Although the cause of the incident is unknown, a v a r _ _ t _

14) of strange t h e _ r _ _ s have been suggested over

15) the _ e _ _ s, including the possibility of extraterrestrial interference!

16) Some people have attempted to find r a _ i _ n _ l explanations

for the mysteries associated with the stretch of water, such as human error or faulty

17) equipment. However, others prefer to b e l _ _ _ e that strange energy

18) fields or supernatural factors have _ _ u s _ d the large number of

19) _ n _ s _ _ l occurrences.

Whether you think that little green men use the Bermuda Triangle as their

20) playground, or conclude that it's just a coincidence, no one can _ e _ y that

21) the mysterious tales have made the triangle one of the most _ u _ i o _ s

stretches of water on the planet.

Stop — you may check your answers in this section only

Section 3: Verbal Reasoning — Odd One Out

Example Read this example question. You may return to this example at any time as you work through this section.

Three of the words in each list are linked.
Mark the rectangle under the word that is **not** related to these three.

A) sister   brother   family   cousin
   ☐   ☐   ▄   ☐

⚠ Wait until you are told to go on ⚠

⏱ You have 6 minutes to complete this section ⏱

There are **18** questions in this section

Three of the words in each list are linked.
Mark the rectangle under the word that is **not** related to these three.

1) draft   chart   table   graph
   ☐   ☐   ☐   ☐

2) grow   expand   swell   ripe
   ☐   ☐   ☐   ☐

3) elated   merry   wistful   overjoyed
   ☐   ☐   ☐   ☐

4) amalgamate   consolidate   blend   disconnect
   ☐   ☐   ☐   ☐

5) dictionary   encyclopedia   novel   thesaurus
   ☐   ☐   ☐   ☐

6) aluminium   lead   steel   granite
   ☐   ☐   ☐   ☐

7) stir   mix   shake   whisk
   ☐   ☐   ☐   ☐

8 crimson ☐   violet ☐   lilac ☐   mauve ☐

9 butterfly ☐   dragonfly ☐   hornet ☐   moth ☐

10 clasp ☐   buckle ☐   zip ☐   seam ☐

11 classroom ☐   bathroom ☐   bedroom ☐   living room ☐

12 demand ☐   receive ☐   request ☐   ask ☐

13 blurred ☐   pixelated ☐   complicated ☐   obscured ☐

14 birch ☐   oak ☐   rose ☐   sycamore ☐

15 triangle ☐   cube ☐   square ☐   rectangle ☐

16 aunt ☐   grandmother ☐   sister ☐   father ☐

17 scowl ☐   frown ☐   grin ☐   glare ☐

18 dishevelled ☐   awkward ☐   clumsy ☐   inelegant ☐

Stop — you may check your answers in this section only

Section 4: Verbal Reasoning — Antonyms

Example Read this example question. You may return to this example at any time as you work through this section.

Choose the word which means the opposite, or nearly the opposite, of the word on the left.

A) **hot** angry ☐ cough ☐ cold ▬ shiver ☐

 Wait until you are told to go on

 You have 6 minutes to complete this section

There are **18** questions in this section

Choose the word which means the opposite, or nearly the opposite, of the word on the left.

1) **upbeat** realistic ☐ pessimistic ☐ derisive ☐ idealistic ☐

2) **significant** superficial ☐ important ☐ superlative ☐ common ☐

3) **limited** finite ☐ comprehensive ☐ general ☐ adequate ☐

4) **maintain** perpetuate ☐ neglect ☐ predicament ☐ continue ☐

5) **conceited** arrogant ☐ generous ☐ helpful ☐ humble ☐

6) **tranquil** congenial ☐ disturbed ☐ peaceful ☐ invigorating ☐

7) **selfish** pensive ☐ obnoxious ☐ magnanimous ☐ understanding ☐

8. **stubborn** — awkward ☐   reasonable ☐   selfless ☐   prudent ☐

9. **acceptance** — importance ☐   dislike ☐   unpopularity ☐   disapproval ☐

10. **clear** — perplexing ☐   illusory ☐   difficult ☐   understood ☐

11. **assured** — calm ☐   reserved ☐   agitated ☐   mild ☐

12. **lively** — active ☐   tired ☐   lethargic ☐   callous ☐

13. **cowardly** — strong ☐   daring ☐   powerful ☐   energetic ☐

14. **nervous** — stressed ☐   prepared ☐   composed ☐   disinterested ☐

15. **contribute** — supply ☐   disperse ☐   original ☐   withdraw ☐

16. **organised** — damaged ☐   obscured ☐   chaotic ☐   dirty ☐

17. **detach** — bind ☐   isolate ☐   rectify ☐   renovate ☐

18. **necessary** — valid ☐   superfluous ☐   extreme ☐   inept ☐

 Stop — you may check your answers in this section only

Section 5: Non-Verbal Reasoning

Example — Read this example question. You may return to this example at any time as you work through this section.

A Work out which 3D figure has been rotated to make the new 3D figure.

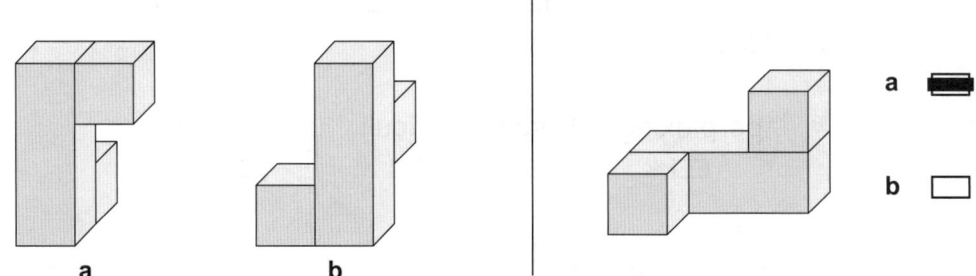

B Work out which set of blocks can be put together to make the 3D figure on the left.

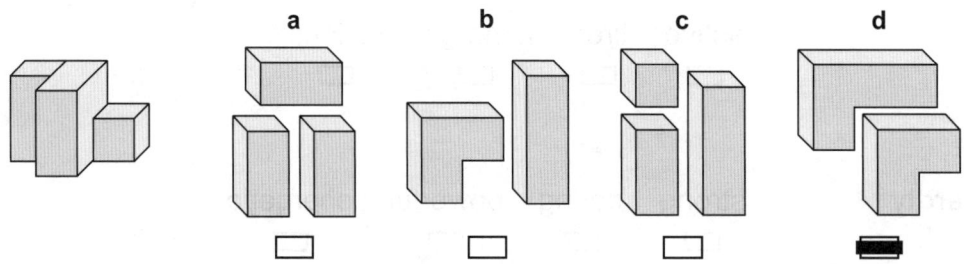

C Work out which option is a top-down 2D view of the 3D figure on the left.

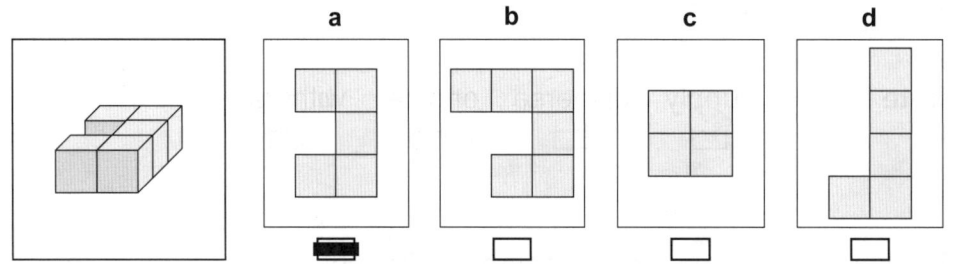

D Work out which of the four cubes can be made from the net.

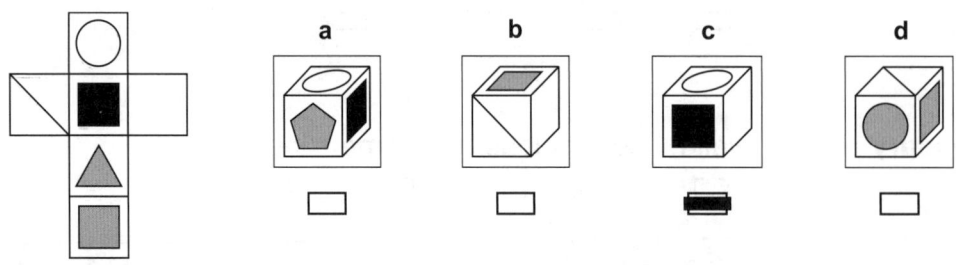

Wait until you are told to go on

You have 9 minutes to complete this section

There are 18 questions in this section

Work out which 3D figure (a, b, c, d, e or f) has been rotated to make the new 3D figure.

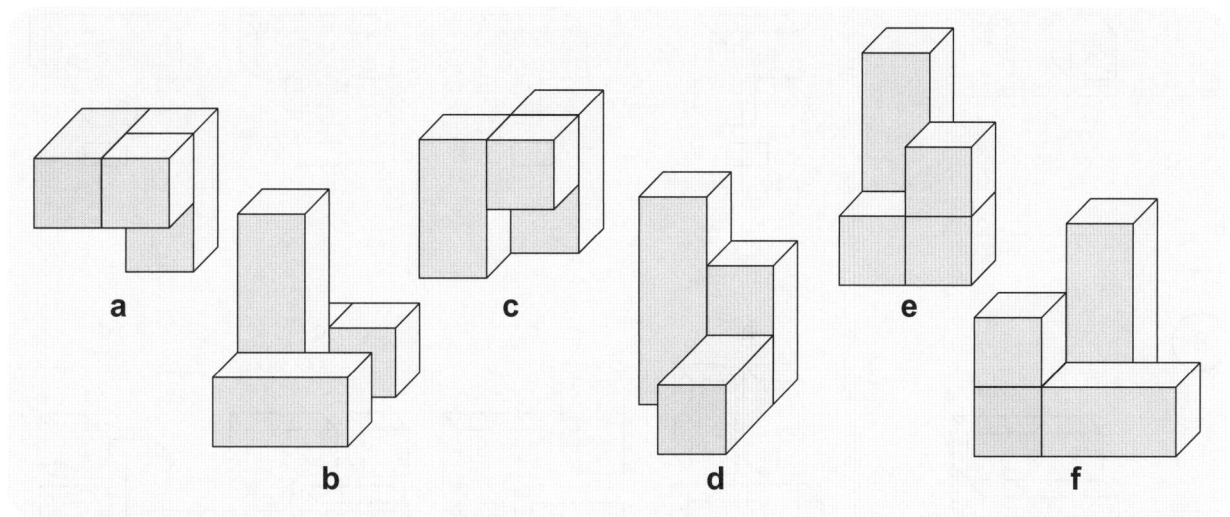

①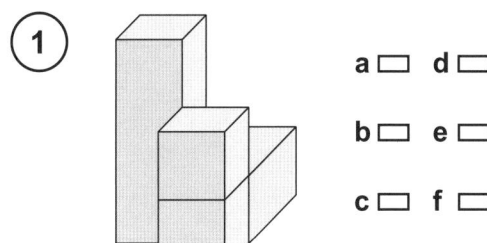
a ☐ d ☐
b ☐ e ☐
c ☐ f ☐

②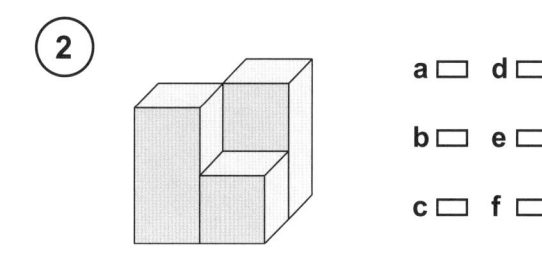
a ☐ d ☐
b ☐ e ☐
c ☐ f ☐

③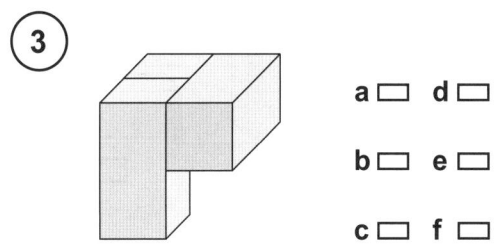
a ☐ d ☐
b ☐ e ☐
c ☐ f ☐

④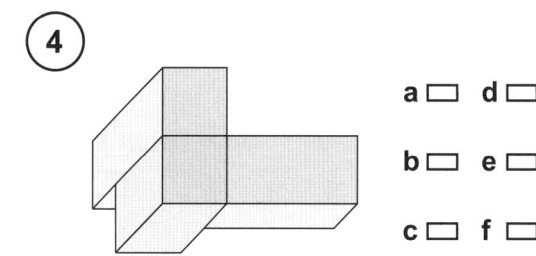
a ☐ d ☐
b ☐ e ☐
c ☐ f ☐

⑤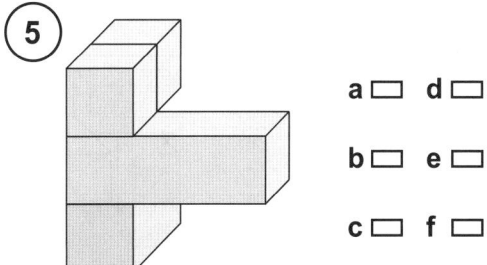
a ☐ d ☐
b ☐ e ☐
c ☐ f ☐

⑥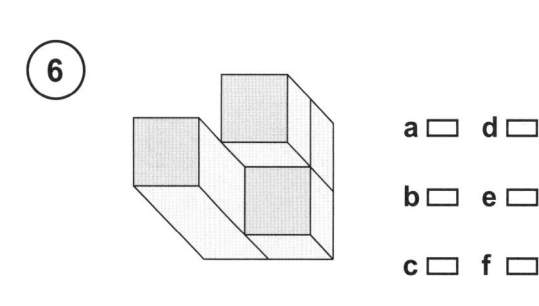
a ☐ d ☐
b ☐ e ☐
c ☐ f ☐

Go to the next question

Work out which set of blocks can be put together to make the 3D figure on the left.

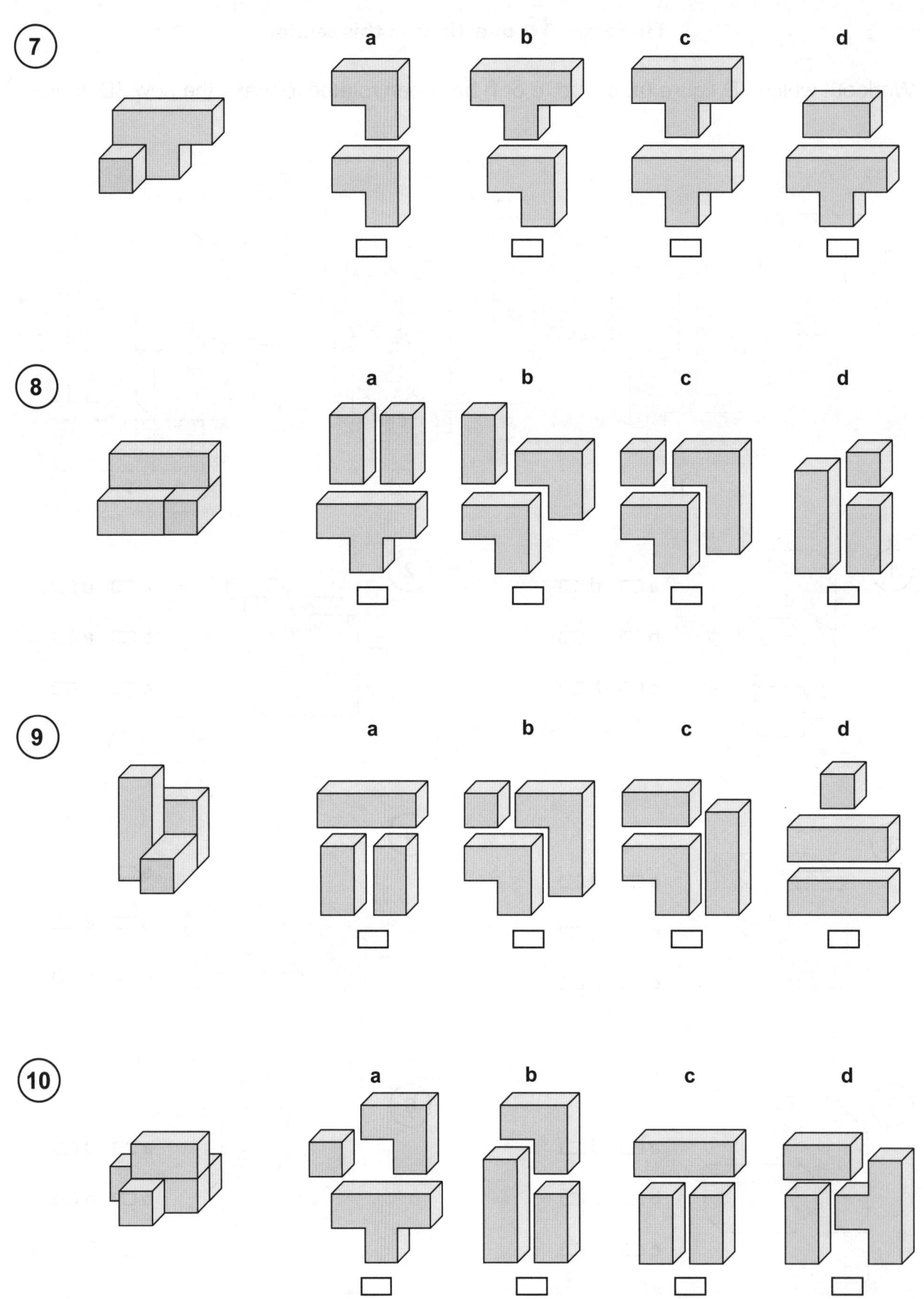

Work out which option is a top-down 2D view of the 3D figure on the left.

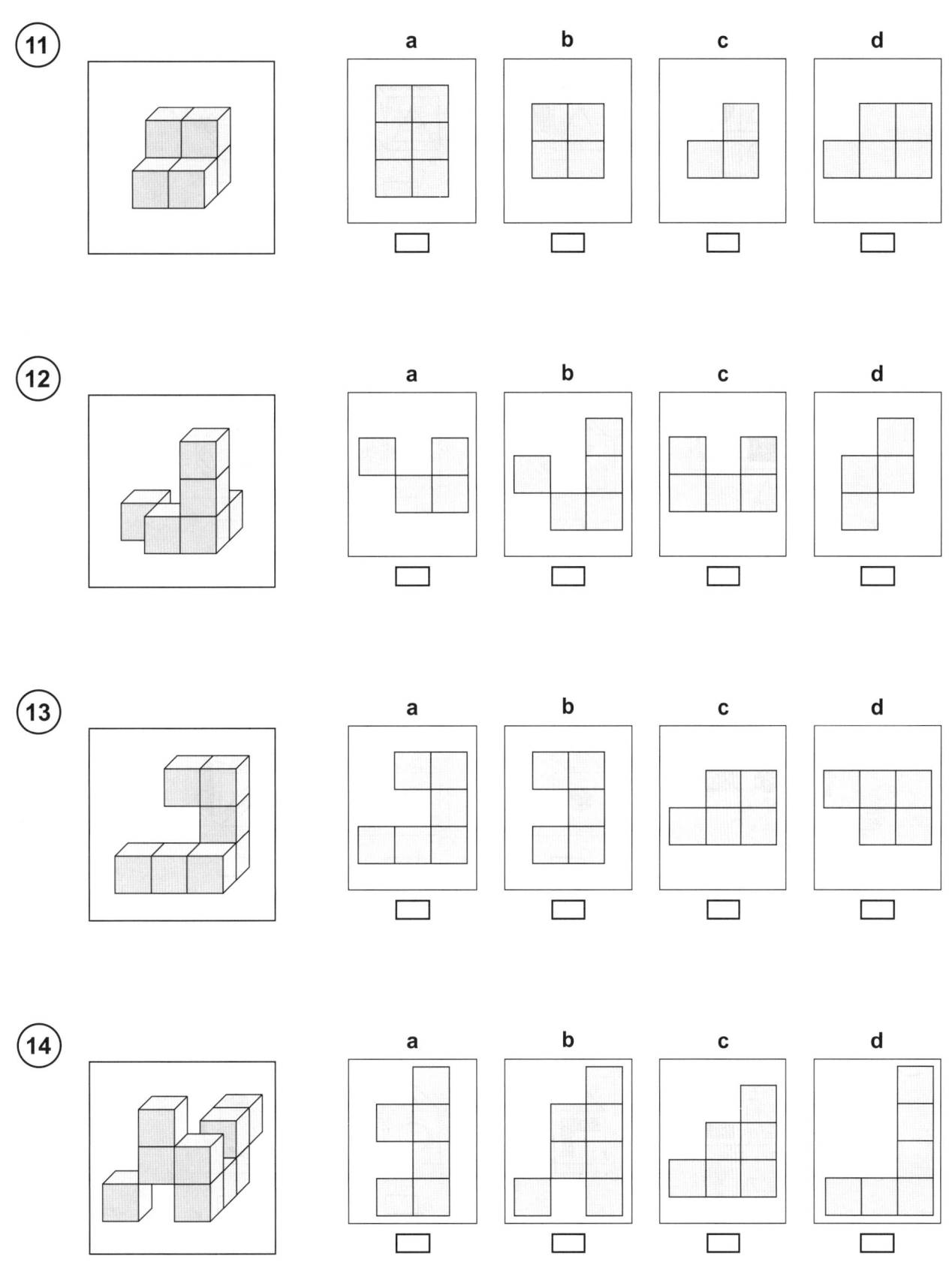

Work out which of the four cubes can be made from the net.

15 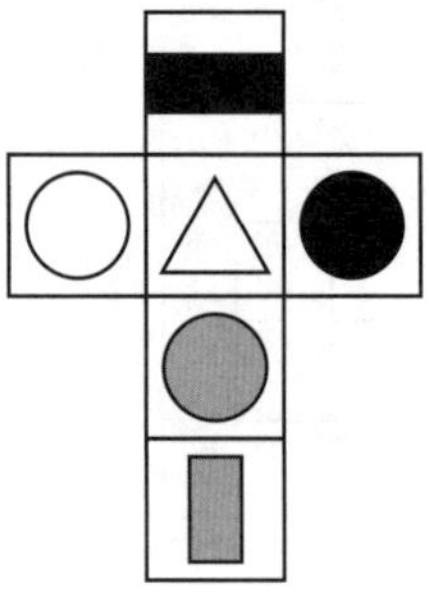

a 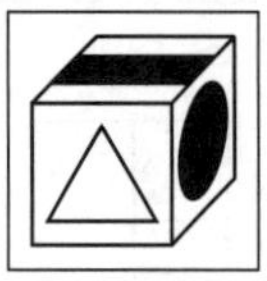

b 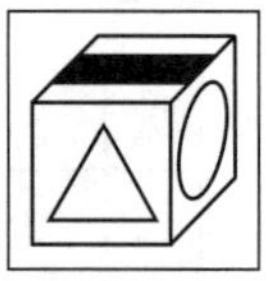

c 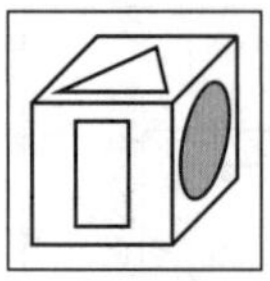

d 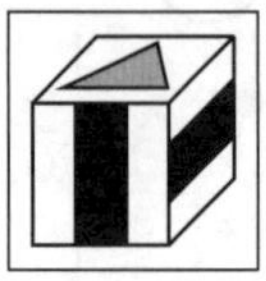

16 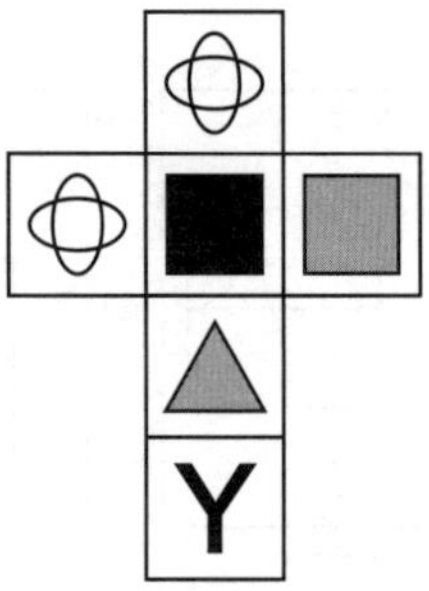

a 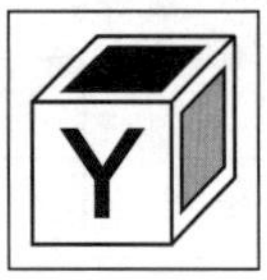

b 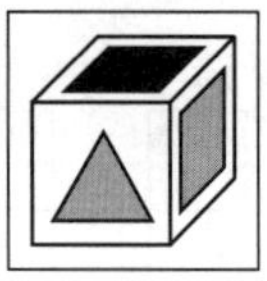

c 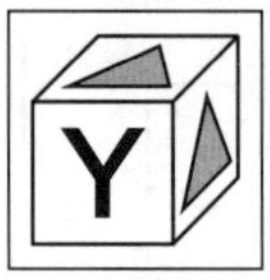

d 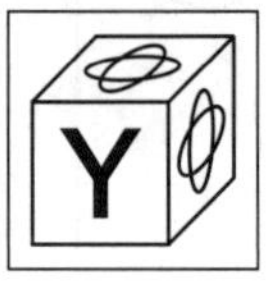

17 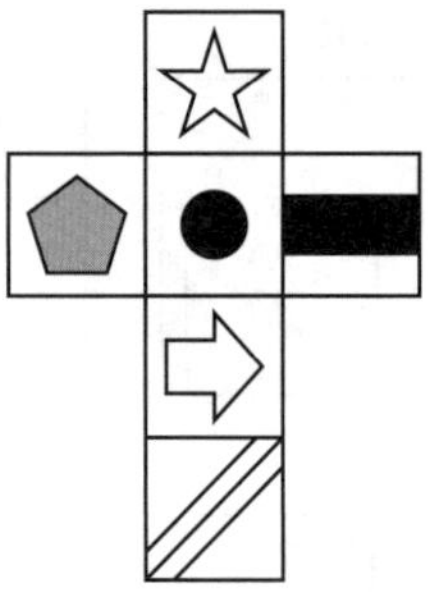

a 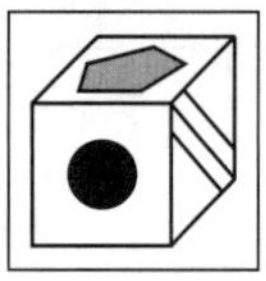

b 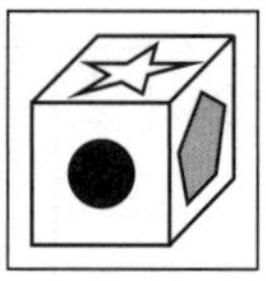

c 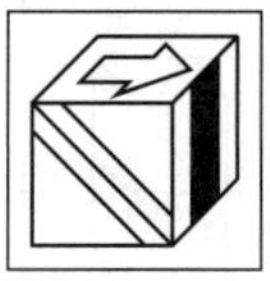

d 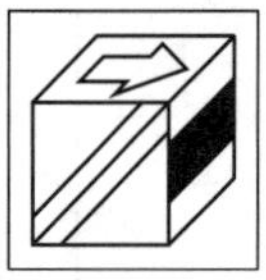

18 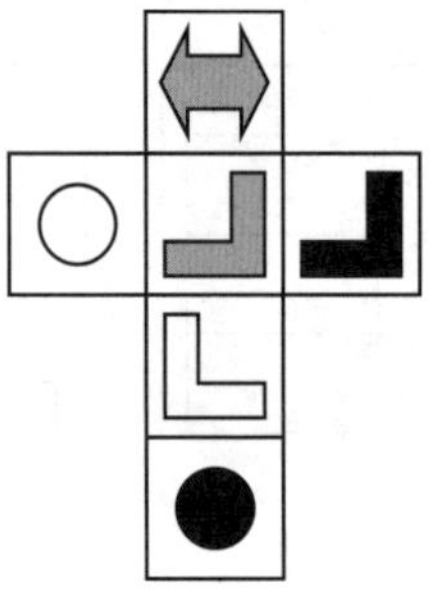

a 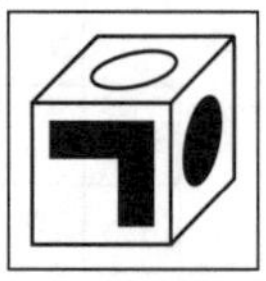

b 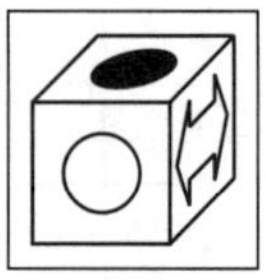

c 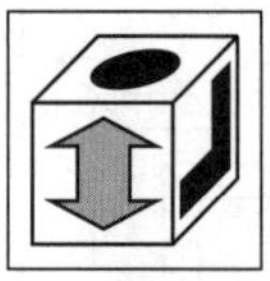

d 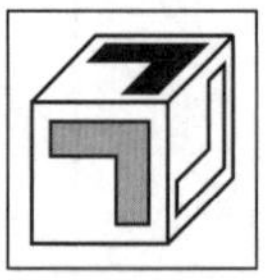

CGP

11+ Practice Paper

For Ages 10-11

Set B: Paper 2
For the CEM Test

Read the following:

Do not open this booklet or start the test until you are told to do so.

1. This test can be taken in either multiple-choice or write-in format.

2. If you are taking it as a multiple-choice test, you should mark your answer to each question in pencil on the separate answer sheet. Mark the correct box quickly and neatly using a horizontal line.

3. If you are taking it as a write-in test, you should write your answer to each question in pencil on the paper. Write your answer carefully in the space provided or, if there is a range of options, mark the correct box quickly and neatly using a horizontal line.

4. If you make a mistake, rub it out and mark your new answer clearly.

5. There are three sections in this test.

6. The time allowed for each section is given at the start of that section. You will have a total of 45 minutes to complete the timed sections of the test.

7. Each section includes examples showing you how to answer the questions. You may refer to these examples at any time as you work through the section.

8. Do as many questions as you can. For some questions you will be given a range of options — if you get stuck on one of these questions, choose the answer that you think is most likely to be correct, then move on to the next question. If you get stuck on a question for which no options are given, leave it and move on to the next question. If you have time at the end of the section, go back and have another go at the questions you could not answer.

9. You should do any rough working on a separate piece of paper.

Work carefully, but go as quickly as you can.

Section 1: Numerical Reasoning

Example Read these example questions. You may return to these examples at any time as you work through this section.

A George draws a graph showing a flight by his remote-control model plane.

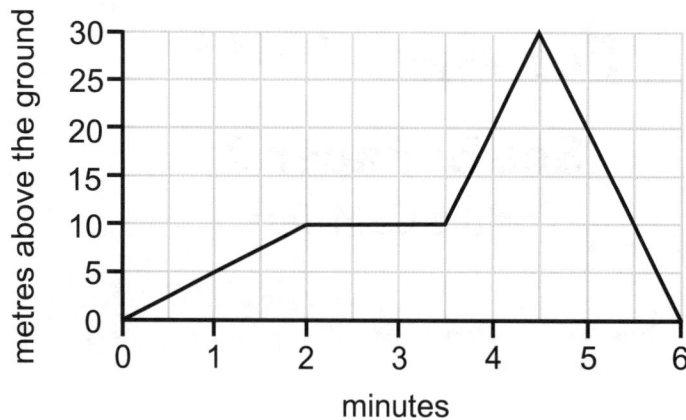

A1 How long did the flight last? `6` minutes

A2 How high was the plane after 4 minutes of flight? `2` `0` m

A3 According to the graph, what was the plane doing between 3½ and 4½ minutes of flight?

speeding up ☐ rising ▬ slowing down ☐ falling ☐

⚠ **Wait until you are told to go on** ⚠

You have 34 minutes to complete this section

There are 14 multi-part questions in this section

1) Jamila goes fruit picking at Fruity Tooty's Pick Your Own.
She picks a selection of apples, pears and plums. She puts them in punnets of 12.

In total, Jamila fills 3½ punnets of apples, 4 punnets of pears and 2¼ punnets of plums.

    a) How many apples did Jamila pick?

    b) How many more pears did Jamila pick than plums?

    c) What is the ratio of pears to apples?
        Express your answer in its simplest form.

The prices of Fruity Tooty's Pick Your Own are in the table below.

Fruit	Price per ¼ punnet
Apple	30p
Pear	50p
Plum	60p
Discount of 20p per full punnet	

    d) How much did Jamila spend on plums?

Go to the next question

2) Derren has a normal pack of 52 playing cards. It contains two red suits — hearts and diamonds, and two black suits — spades and clubs.
The cards are numbered Ace, 2, 3, 4, 5, 6, 7, 8, 9, 10, Jack, Queen and King.

Hearts

Spades

Diamonds

Clubs

a) Derren removes the King of Diamonds from the pack of cards and puts it aside. What fraction of the remaining cards are either a King or Queen?

$3/52$ ☐ $7/51$ ☐ $7/52$ ☐ $3/51$ ☐ $4/51$ ☐

b) Derren removes the following 5 cards from the whole pack of cards and puts them aside.

What fraction of the remaining cards are red?

$47/52$ ☐ $12/13$ ☐ $5/6$ ☐ $22/47$ ☐ $1/52$ ☐

c) Derren takes the whole pack of cards and removes 12 cards.
He looks through the remaining cards and works out that $1/20$ of the remaining cards in the pack are Aces.
How many Aces have been removed in the 12 cards?

3) The diagram below shows the dimensions of a fish tank.

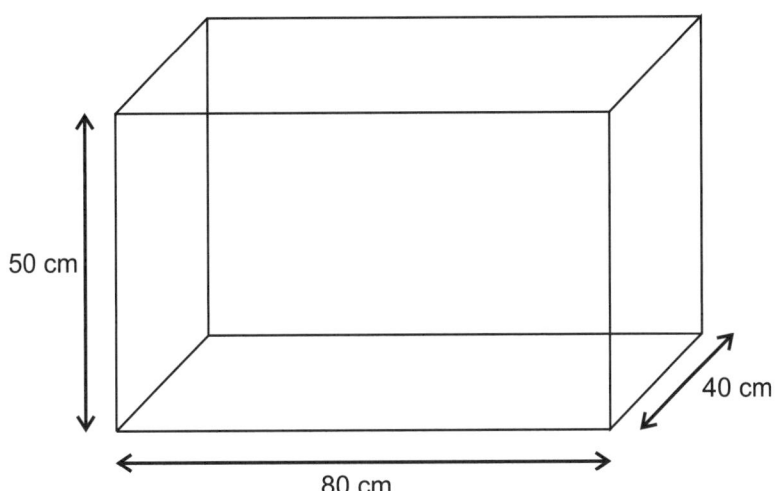

a) What is the total capacity of the tank in cm³?

 cm³

b) Kim fills the tank ¾ full. How many cm³ of water are in the fish tank?

 cm³

c) 1000 cm³ = 1 litre. How many litres of water are there in the fish tank?

12 litres   160 litres   4 litres   120 litres   16 litres
  ☐   ☐   ☐   ☐   ☐

d) Kim allows 10 litres of water per fish in the tank.
   How many fish will Kim be able to keep in the tank?

④ The map below shows a path through a wood.
5 children are standing at different points on the path.
Each square on the map corresponds to 1 metre.

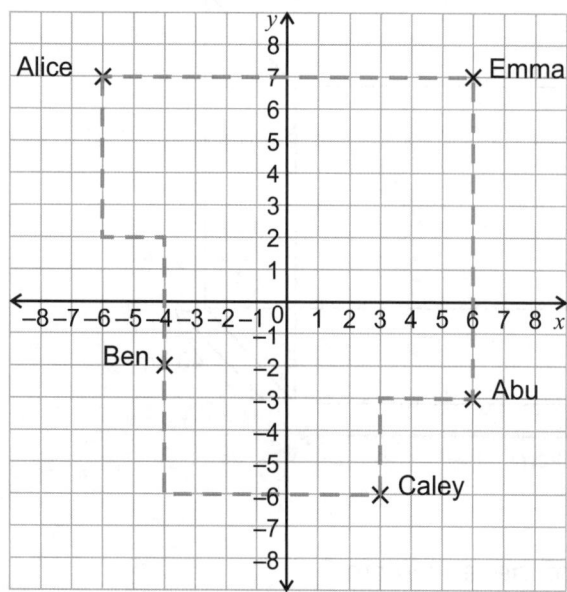

All 5 children run at different paces:

Name	Speed
Alice	6 metres per second
Ben	2 metres per second
Caley	0.5 metres per second
Abu	4 metres per second
Emma	3 metres per second

a) Ben starts running in a clockwise direction.
He runs for 10 seconds. What are the coordinates of the point he arrives at?

(3, 7)　　(−6, 6)　　(2, −6)　　(6, 0)　　(7, 3)

b) Emma starts running in a clockwise direction. After 1 second Abu sets off in an anticlockwise direction. At what point will they meet?

(6, 1)　　(1, 6)　　(−1, −6)　　(6, 4)　　(6, 2)

c) Caley and Alice both start running in an anticlockwise direction.
At what point will Alice catch up with Caley?

(−4, 3)　　(5, −3)　　(−6, −1)　　(3, −4)　　(−6, 3)

5) The picture below shows a rectangular lunch box.
It is divided into 4 segments: 3 triangles and 1 quadrilateral.

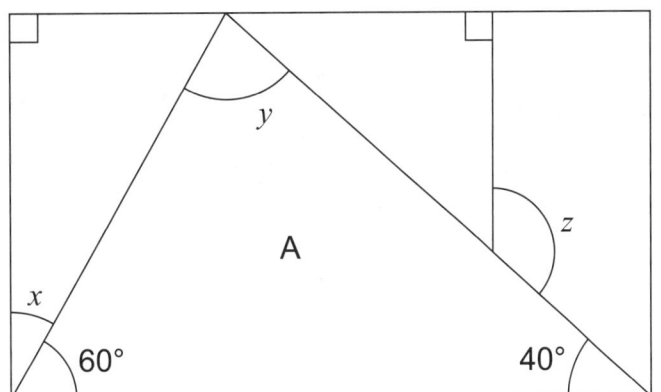

Not drawn accurately

a) What is the size of the angle marked *x*?

⬚⬚⬚ °

b) What is the size of the angle marked *y*?

⬚⬚⬚ °

c) What type of triangle is the shape marked **A**?

scalene ☐   isosceles ☐   right-angled ☐   equilateral ☐

d) What is the size of the angle marked *z*?

⬚⬚⬚ °

Go to the next question ➡

6) Chiara has a photo frame. It is made up of an empty picture space and a border.

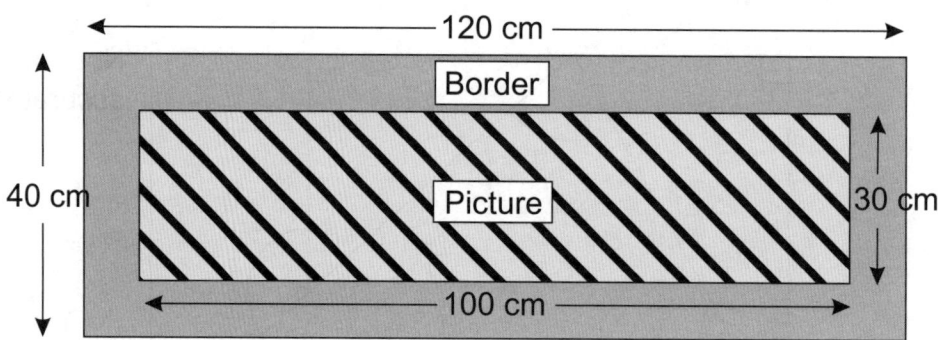

a) What is the area of the border?

 cm²

b) Chiara wants to fill her frame with individual photographs.
The photographs are 6 cm tall and 5 cm wide.
How many photographs will she be able to fit in the frame with no overlap and keeping all photos the right way up?

c) Chiara has a smaller frame which exactly fits 40 photographs into the picture space. The photographs are 6 cm tall and 5 cm wide.
What is the area of the picture space?

☐☐☐☐ cm²

d) The total area of the smaller frame is 1725 cm².
What is the area of the border?

☐☐☐☐ cm²

7) Billy asked his classmates what their favourite instrument was. He recorded the results in a pictogram.

Instrument	
Piano	♫♫♫♫♫♫♪
Flute	♫♪
Cello	♫♪
Drums	♫♫♫
Guitar	♫♫♫♪

♫ = 6 children

a) How many people said that the piano was their favourite instrument?

b) How many more people said that guitar was their favourite instrument than said the flute was?

c) How many fewer people said that cello was their favourite instrument than piano?

d) The piano was as popular as which instruments combined?

Drums, Flute and Cello ☐   Drums and Flute ☐   Cello and Flute ☐   Cello, Flute and Guitar ☐   Flute and Guitar ☐

Go to the next question

8) Yusra is measuring the temperature of a cake once a minute from when it comes out of the oven. She puts her results into the table below.

Time (mins)	Temperature (°C)
1	120
2	114
3	108
4	102
5	96

a) Which expression describes the temperature after m minutes?

$120m$ ☐ $120m - m$ ☐ $126 - 6m$ ☐ $126 - 2m$ ☐ $120 - m$ ☐

b) What will be the temperature of the cake after 11 minutes?

 °C

c) Yusra needs to wait until the cake is 30 °C or below before she can ice it. How many minutes will Yusra need to wait until she can ice the cake?

 minutes

9) A school pays £70 to print 100 copies of the school magazine.
The school sells 90 copies for £1.50 each.

a) What is the profit after paying for the printing of all 100 copies?

£ ☐☐☐

b) Class A spends £45 on school magazines.
If each child has bought one magazine, how many children are in Class A?

☐☐

c) The school increases the price of the school magazine by 20%.
How much will Class A spend in total if they
buy one copy each at the new price?

£ ☐☐

Go to the next question

10) Franz, Ollie and Xia all own dogs. They are looking at hiring one of four different dog walking companies. All four companies charge depending on the number of dogs, d, and the length of the walk in miles, m.

Company	Price
Pooch Pals	$10d + m$
Barking Buddies	$2dm$
Canine Companions	$4(d + m)$
Happy Tails	$(5dm) \div 2$

a) Franz owns two dogs. He wants them to be taken on a 5 mile walk. How much will it cost Franz if he goes with Canine Companions?

£ ☐☐.☐☐

b) Ollie owns three dogs. He wants them to be taken on a 4 mile walk. How much will it cost Ollie if he goes with Happy Tails?

£ ☐☐.☐☐

c) Xia owns five dogs. She wants them to be taken on a 6 mile walk. Which company will be the cheapest for Xia?

Pooch Pals ☐   Barking Buddies ☐   Canine Companions ☐   Happy Tails ☐

d) Xia pays Pooch Pals £58 to take her five dogs for a walk. How long was the walk that her dogs were taken on?

☐☐☐ miles

11) Below is a bus timetable for the trip from Didford to Plymstone.
The scheduled journey time for the bus is always the same.

Didford	10:15	10:45	11:15
Topham	10:31	11:01	11:31
Sidton	10:44	?	11:44
Dawcombe	11:00	11:30	12:00
Ide	11:20	11:50	12:20
Halldon	11:43	12:13	12:43
Plymstone	11:59	12:29	12:59

a) At what time will the 10:45 bus from Didford arrive at Sidton?

b) How many minutes does it take to get from Halldon to Plymstone on the bus?

_____ minutes

c) Lydia gets on the bus at 11:01 in Topham. She stays on for 72 minutes before getting off. At which stop did Lydia get off the bus?

Sidton   Dawcombe   Ide   Halldon   Plymstone

d) The bus that leaves Didford at 11:15 gets stuck in a traffic jam between Sidton and Ide. There is a 15 minute delay between Sidton and Dawcombe, and a further 8 minute delay between Dawcombe and Ide.
At what time will the 11:15 bus arrive in Ide?

Go to the next question

12 Zhi goes on a run. He runs along a straight track away from his house and back. He plots a graph of how far he ran against the time.

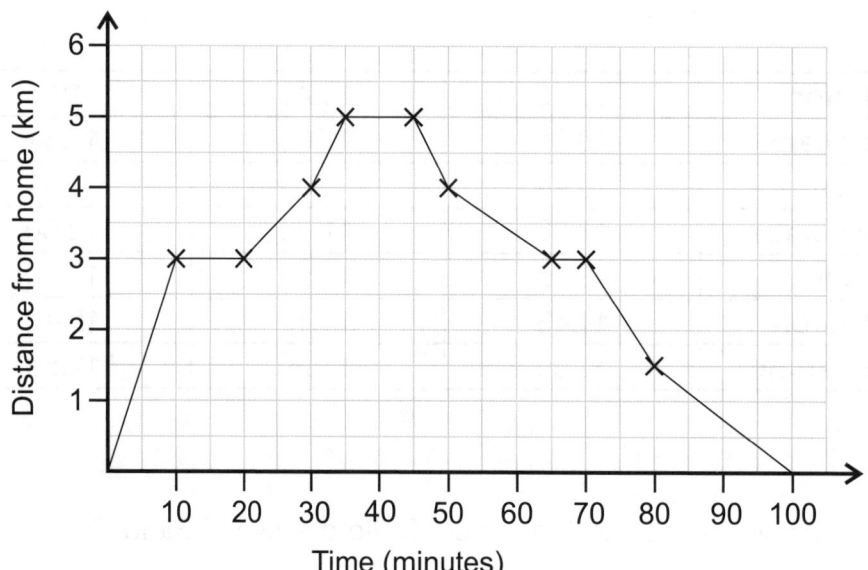

a) How long was Zhi's run?

☐☐ km

b) For how many minutes did Zhi rest on his run?

☐☐ minutes

c) Between what times did Zhi run the fastest?

| 0 – 10 minutes | 20 – 30 minutes | 45 – 50 minutes | 70 – 80 minutes | 80 – 100 minutes |
| ☐ | ☐ | ☐ | ☐ | ☐ |

13 The menu for the Merry Cow Milkshake Parlour is shown below. The price of a milkshake depends on the size and the number and type of toppings.

Size	
Small	£2.00
Medium	£3.00
Large	£3.50
Huge	£3.80

Standard Toppings (+ 20p each)	Deluxe Toppings (+ 50p each)
Strawberries, Cherries, Chocolate chips, Granola, Banana, Marshmallows	Brownies, Passion fruit, Chocolate flake, Sherbet, Fudge, Blueberries

a) Jake buys a large milkshake with strawberries, fudge and blueberries. How much does this cost him?

£ 04.70

b) Katie buys a medium milkshake with a number of standard and deluxe toppings. She pays £4.10. How many standard toppings did she chose?

3

On Mondays, there is a special discount of 20% off all sizes of milkshakes, and 50% off all toppings.

c) Sadaf buys a small milkshake with cherries, brownies and sherbet toppings. How much will this cost her on a Monday?

£ 02.20

Go to the next question

14) Farmer Charles owns 450 acres of land.
He is dividing it up between different crops and animals.
He makes the table below to show how much of
the total land each animal or crop will have.

Animal/Crop	Land assigned
Barley	20%
Wheat	7/50
Cows	45%
Maize	45 acres
Sheep	11%

a) How many acres has Farmer Charles assigned to sheep?

☐☐.☐ acres

b) How many acres has Farmer Charles assigned to wheat?

☐☐ acres

c) What is the proportion of land that Farmer Charles has assigned to maize as a percentage?

☐☐ %

d) Which animal or crop has the fewest acres?

Barley ☐   Wheat ☐   Cows ☐   Maize ☐   Sheep ☐

Stop — you may check your answers in this section only

BLANK PAGE

Section 2: Verbal Reasoning — Cloze

Example Read these example questions. You may return to these examples at any time as you work through this section.

Tea is often thought of as a traditional English drink. (A) ☐ Despite / ■ However / ☐ Also / ☐ While, it was popular in China centuries before it (B) ☐ brought / ☐ drunk / ☐ travelled / ■ arrived in Europe.

Wait until you are told to go on

You have 5 minutes to complete this section

There are 14 questions in this section

Today, people all over the world (1) ☐ use / ☐ take / ☐ find / ☐ select phones for granted.

However, the first practical telephone wasn't (2) ☐ invented / ☐ found / ☐ discovered / ☐ allowed until the late nineteenth century. Alexander Graham Bell was awarded a (3) ☐ patent / ☐ design / ☐ pattern / ☐ study for the telephone in 1876. Bell's telephone was very (4) ☐ akin / ☐ similar / ☐ different / ☐ unlike to those we use today. It was much bigger, and definitely not (5) ☐ portable / ☐ cumbersome / ☐ substantial / ☐ hefty !

Bell's (6) ☐ research ☐ knowledge ☐ discovery ☐ examination on hearing, elocution and speech was

(7) ☐ influenced ☐ widened ☐ diminished ☐ supplemented by the fact that his mother and wife were both deaf.

He experimented with other hearing devices before he (8) ☐ customised ☐ created ☐ abolished ☐ organised the telephone. The first comprehensive sentence that Bell said (9) ☐ by ☐ on ☐ next ☐ with his telephone was "Mr Watson...come here...I want to see you."

(10) ☐ Within ☐ During ☐ Although ☐ For ten years, more than 150 000 people in America owned telephones, but Bell refused to have a telephone in (11) ☐ his ☐ him ☐ he ☐ its own study because he thought it would make him less (12) ☐ discreet ☐ imaginative ☐ intelligent ☐ productive .

Although Bell (13) ☐ knew ☐ thought ☐ understood ☐ considered his telephone would be a distraction, these days most people regard phones as an (14) ☐ essential ☐ inferior ☐ obligatory ☐ informative part of everyday life.

Stop — you may check your answers in this section only

Section 3: Non-Verbal Reasoning

Example Read these example questions. You may return to these examples at any time as you work through this section.

A Look at how the first two figures are changed, and then work out which option would look like the third figure if you changed it in the same way:

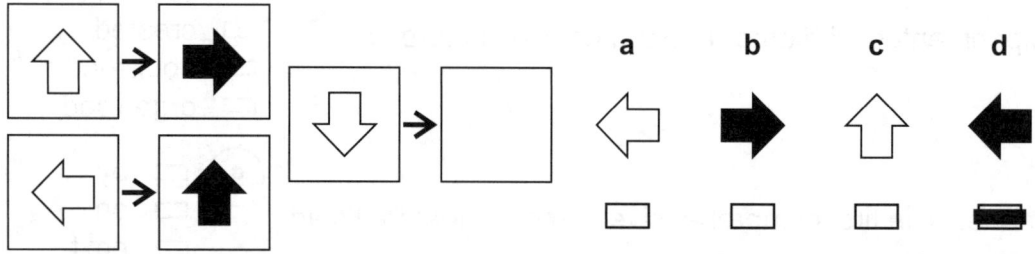

B Work out which of the six hexagons on the right best fits in place of the missing hexagon in the grid:

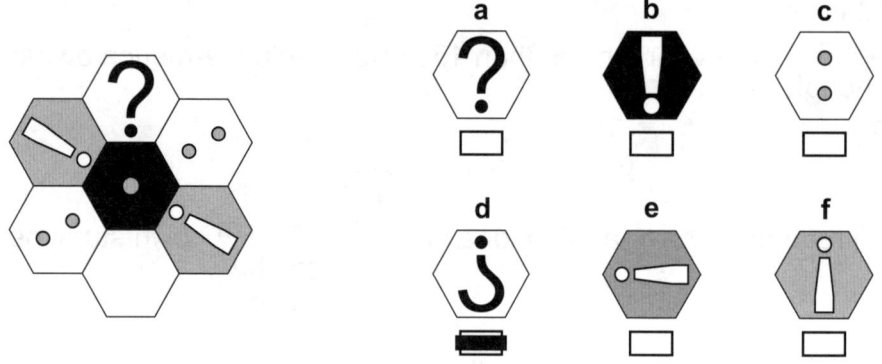

C Work out which option is most like the two figures on the left:

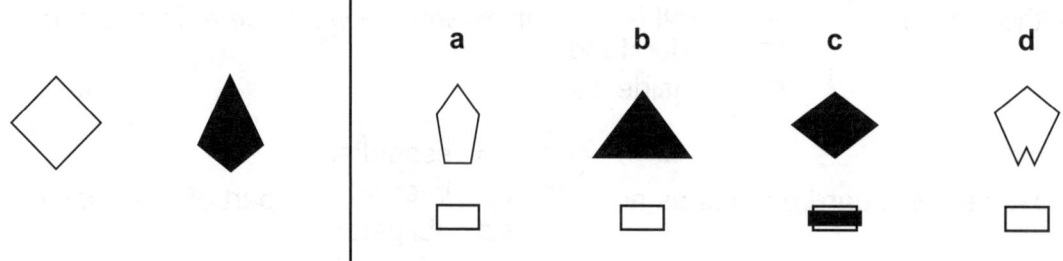

Wait until you are told to go on

You have 6 minutes to complete this section

There are 16 questions in this section

Look at how the first two figures are changed, and then work out which option would look like the third figure if you changed it in the same way:

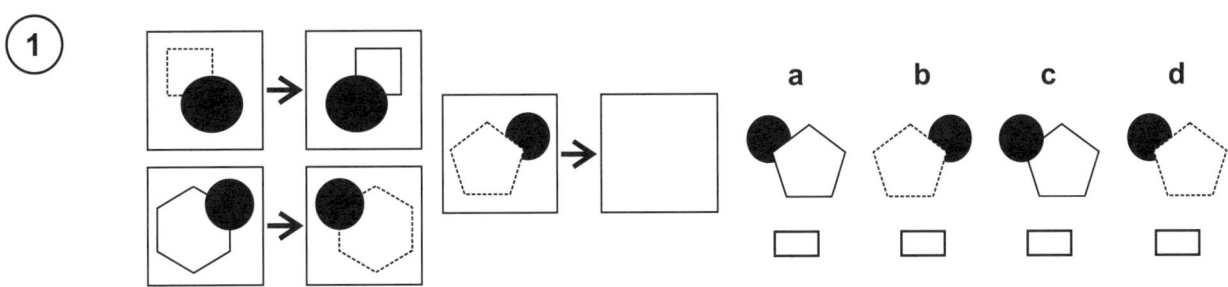

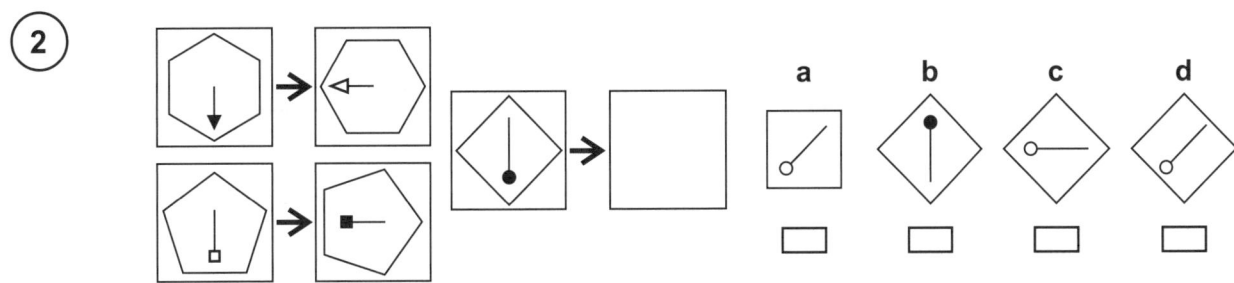

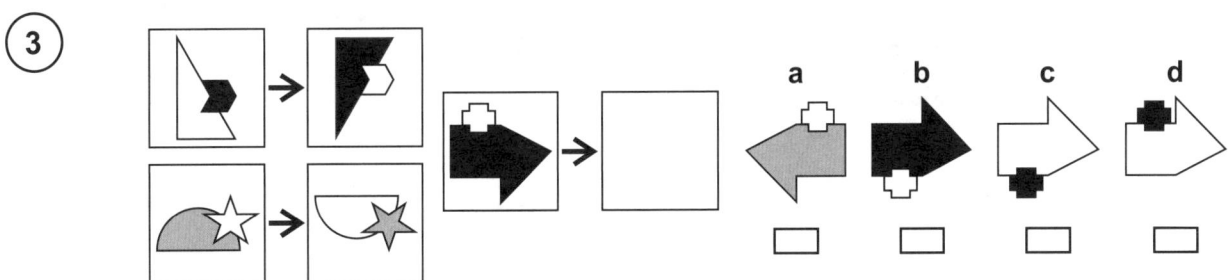

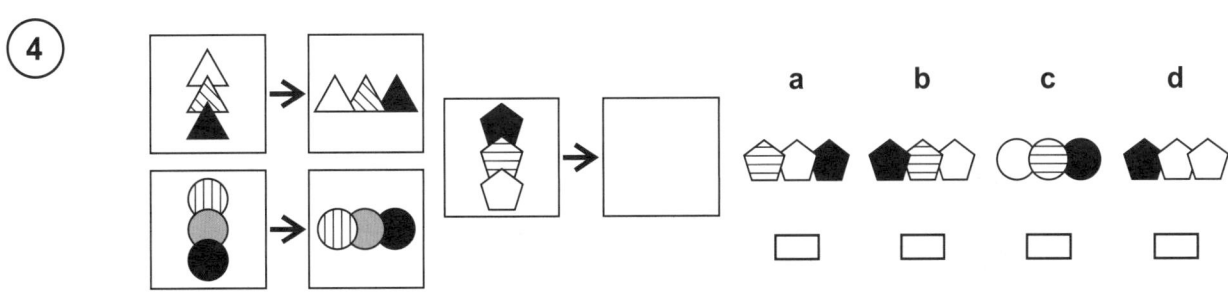

Go to the next question

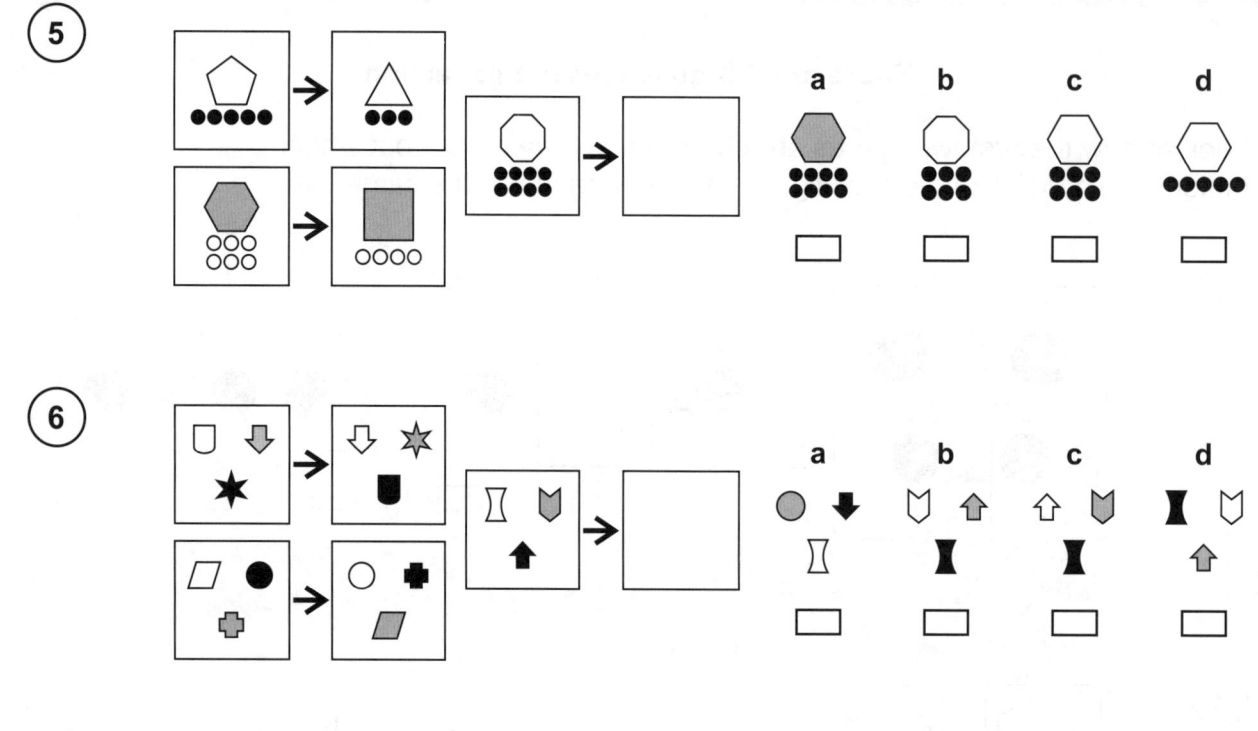

Work out which of the six hexagons on the right best fits in place of the missing hexagon in the grid:

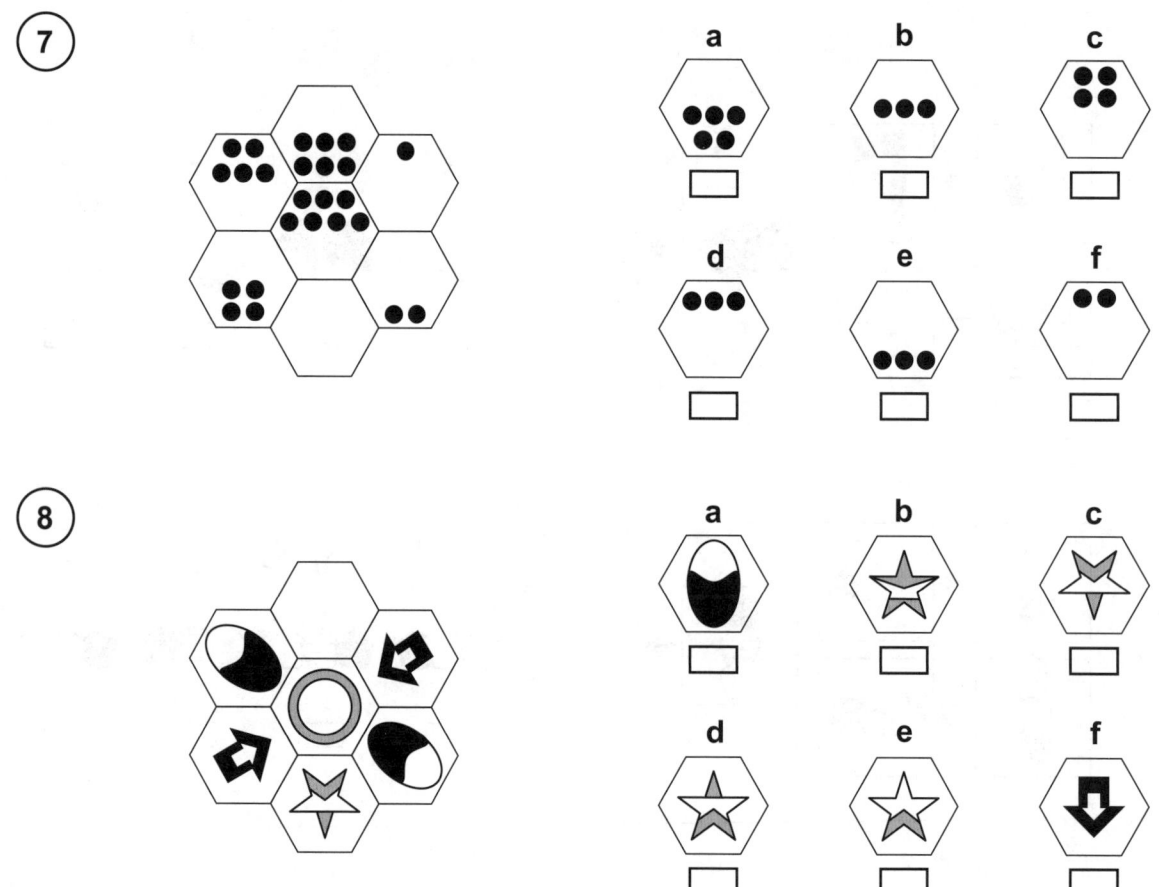

9

10

11

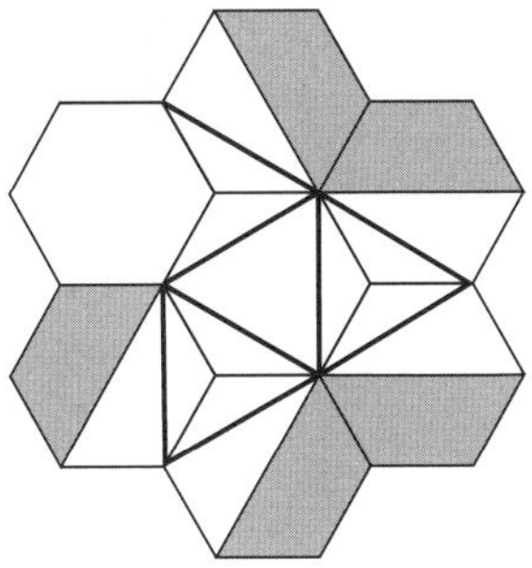

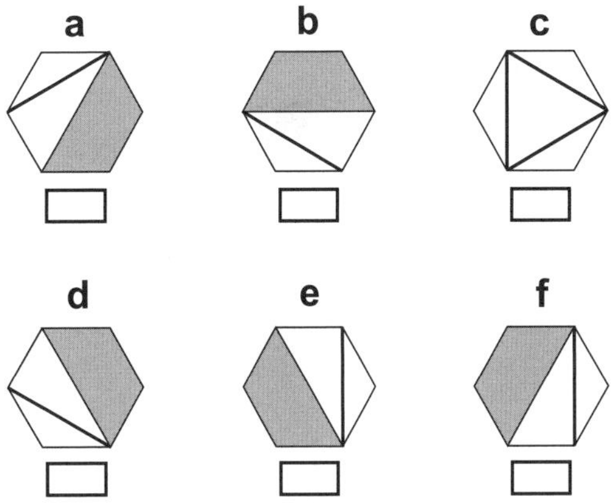

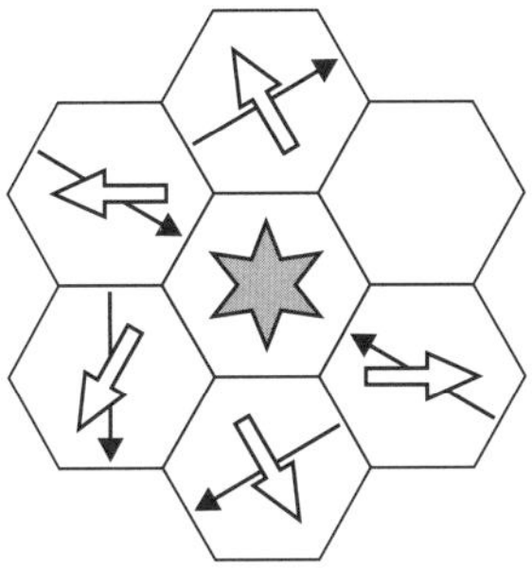

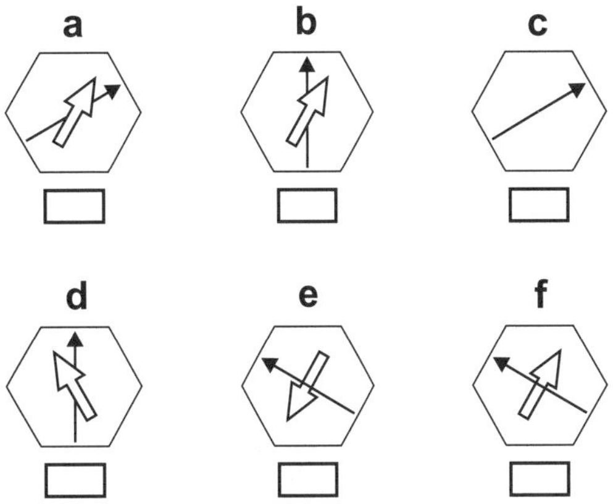

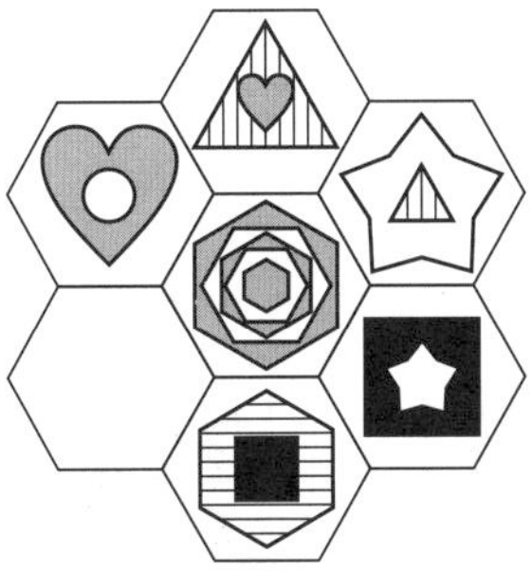

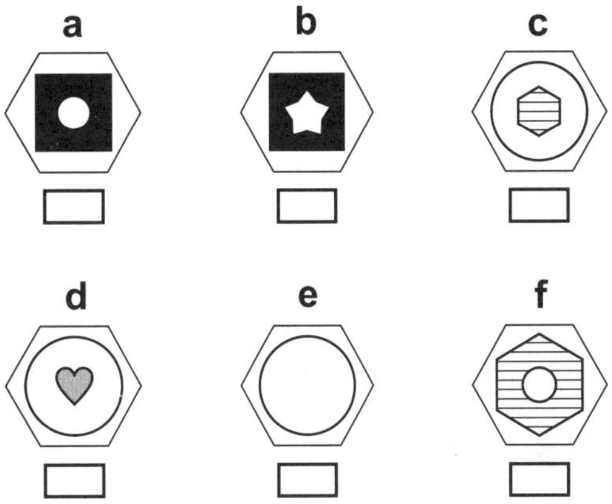

Work out which option is most like the two figures on the left:

12

Go to the next question

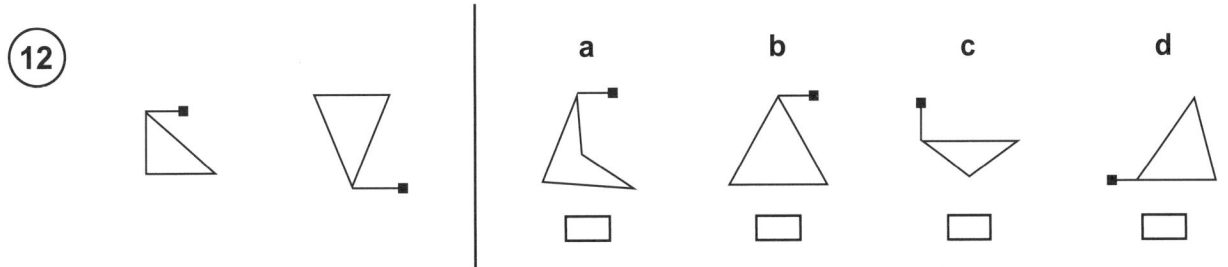

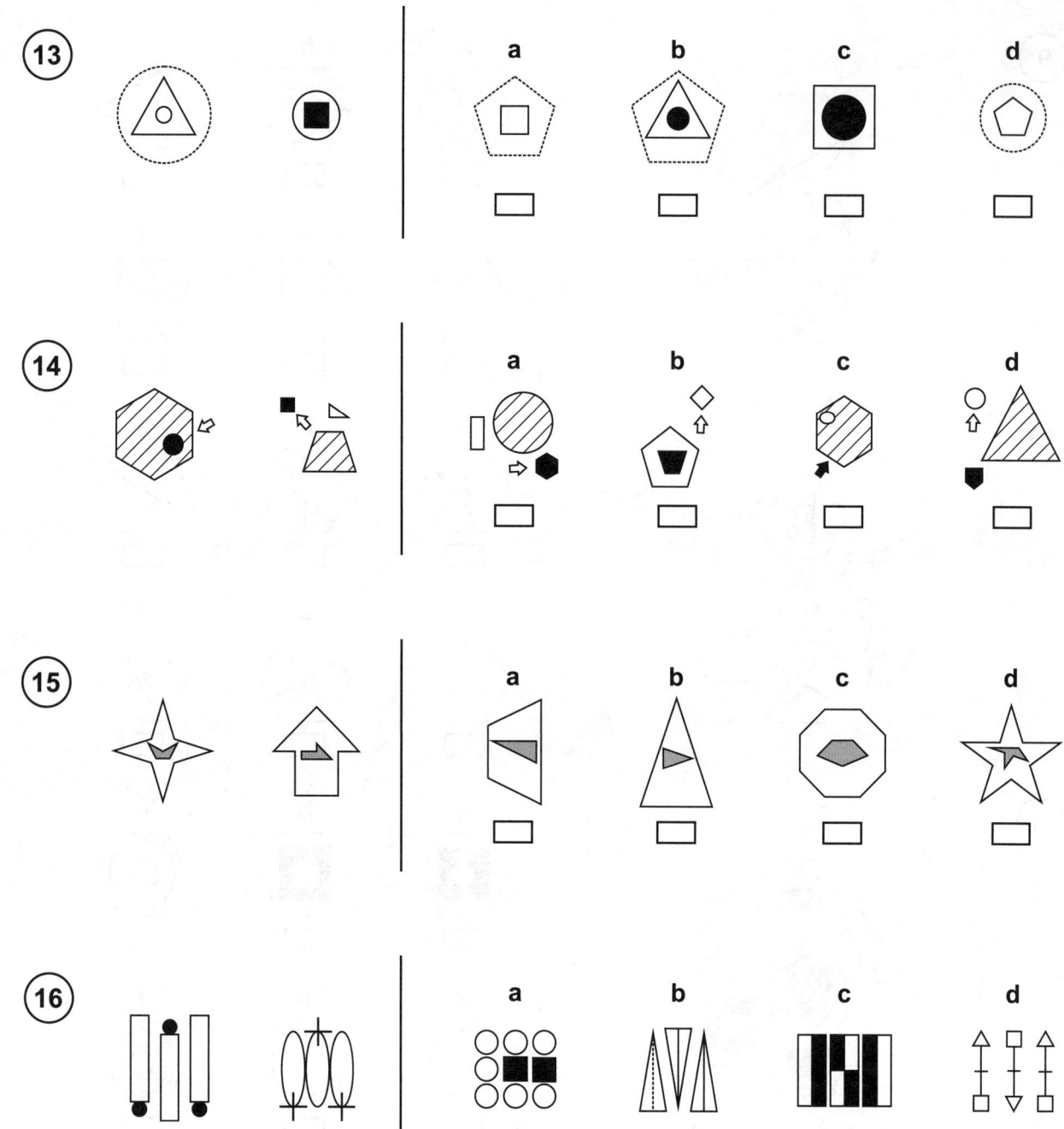

CGP

11+ Practice Papers

For the CEM test

Answer Book

Ages 10-11

Pack 2

Set A — Paper 1

Section 1: Verbal Reasoning — Comprehension 1: Don't get in a spin

1) C
The text says that track bikes are "similar to road bikes". Road bikes have "curved handlebars", so track bikes don't have straight handlebars.

2) C
In the passage it says that "Cyclists race for 21 days (with a couple of rest days on top of this)". 21 days is the equivalent of three weeks, so the Tour de France lasts for more than three weeks.

3) B
In the passage it says that "getting exercise is a vital part of looking after your health" and that "Riding a bike is one of the easiest ways to build regular exercise into your life". So, according to the author, the main benefit of cycling is that it is good for your health.

4. C
The text says that track bikes "have only one gear", so C is false.

5) D
The use of the word "drag" suggests that the act is forced and emphasises that it can be difficult to make yourself go running.

6) C
In the passage it says that "cycling puts very little strain on ankle, hip and knee joints", which reduces the risk of long-term injuries.

7) A
In the passage it says that BMX bikes "have a single gear", and that road bikes have "low gears" as well as "high gears".

8) A
In the passage it says that many people find it "difficult to make time for exercise". So their busy lifestyles prevent them from exercising.

9) B
In the passage it says that cycling regularly can "improve your fitness and reduce stress". Options 2 and 3 are additional benefits of cycling, not reasons why it's good for your health.

10) C
In the passage it says that cycling causes fewer long-term injuries "compared to high-impact sports such as running".

11) B
In the passage it says that road bikes have "thin, smooth tyres to reduce friction" — if there is less friction between the tyres and the road, then the bike will be able to move faster.

12) D
"professional" refers to something that people do to earn a living.

13) C
"exclusively" means 'solely'.

14) C
"challenging" means 'demanding'.

15) D
A "way of life" means the typical way in which you live, so for some people cycling affects how they live their lives.

16) D
"up for grabs" means available to be won by the best competitors.

Section 2: Verbal Reasoning — Comprehension 2: The History of the Hollywood Sign

1) D
The text says that the sign was "erected by a local businessman" to help him "fill the expensive housing estate he was building", so it was intended as an advertisement.

2) D
The text says that the "letter 'H' had been missing" since "the early 1940s", and the sign wasn't repaired until 1949, when the Hollywood Chamber of Commerce removed the word 'land' from the sign.

3) D
The text says that each letter is between 31 and 40 feet wide, and there are nine letters, so the widest the sign could be in total is 9 × 40 = 360 feet.

4) C
The text says that 2013 was the sign's 90th birthday, so it was erected in 1923. The word 'land' was removed from the sign in 1949, 26 years later.

5) D
The text says that construction began in August 1978 and that there was no sign for "three months", which means the new sign appeared some time in November 1978.

6) B
The text says that the sign cost more than $250 000 to build and that patrons "invested in stronger materials". This suggests that these materials were expensive to source.

7) C
The text says that "In the late 1940s, ownership of the sign was handed over to the city". Before then it was owned by Harry Chandler.

8) C
The text says that "Although they [the Chamber] removed the light bulbs... maintenance costs continued to escalate". This suggests that the bulbs were removed to save money.

9) D
A 'Golden Age' is a time when something is at its peak, so the 1920s are known as the 'Golden Age of Hollywood' because the movie business was very successful then.

10) B
The text says that Harry Chandler "had not meant the sign to last" so "it was not made of the most resilient materials."

Section 3: Verbal Reasoning — Multiple Meanings

1) bank
'bank' can mean 'a place to keep money' or 'the land beside a body of water'.

2) back
'back' can mean 'to support' or 'the reverse'.

3) jar
'jar' can mean 'a food container' or 'annoy'.

4) change
'change' can mean 'a modification' or 'money of relatively low value'.

5) clear
'clear' can mean 'straightforward' or 'prove innocent'.

6) fair
'fair' can mean 'not biased' or 'of light complexion'.

7) purchase
'purchase' can mean 'a grip that prevents something from slipping' or 'acquire with money'.

8) engaged
'engaged' can mean 'promised to be married' or 'in use'.

9) plant
'plant' can mean 'a living organism which grows in the ground' or 'a place where a product is manufactured'.

10) light
'light' can mean 'not serious' or 'not dark'.

11) converse
'converse' can mean 'contrasting' or 'engage in a spoken exchange'.

12) permit
'permit' can mean 'a document which grants authorisation' or 'consent'.

Section 4: Verbal Reasoning — Antonyms

1) trivial
'important' means 'significant', whereas 'trivial' means 'insignificant'.

2) cautious
'careless' means 'not taking care', whereas 'cautious' means 'taking a lot of care'.

3) worldly
'unsophisticated' means 'inexperienced', whereas 'worldly' means 'experienced'.

4) frivolous
'sensible' means 'practical', whereas 'frivolous' means 'impractical'.

5) frail
'tough' means 'strong', whereas 'frail' means 'weak'.

6) foe
'friend' means 'ally', whereas 'foe' means 'enemy'.

7) proven
'theoretical' means 'based on what is believed to be possible', whereas 'proven' means 'shown to be true'.

8) profound
'shallow' means 'lacking depth', whereas 'profound' means 'deep'.

9) mobile
'fixed' means 'immovable', whereas 'mobile' means 'movable'.

10) varied
'uniform' means 'the same', whereas 'varied' means 'different'.

11) quirky
'conventional' means 'normal', whereas 'quirky' means 'eccentric'.

12) flippant
'respectful' refers to taking something seriously, whereas 'flippant' refers to not taking something seriously.

13) passive
'dynamic' means 'active', whereas 'passive' means 'inactive'.

14) arduous
'easy' means 'not difficult', whereas 'arduous' means 'difficult'.

15) loiter
'hurry' means 'rush', whereas 'loiter' means 'dawdle'.

16) forfeit
'award' means 'a prize', whereas 'forfeit' means 'a punishment'.

Section 5: Verbal Reasoning — Synonyms

1) despise
Both words mean 'feel strong dislike'.

2) austere
Both words mean 'plain'.

3) promising
Both words mean 'giving hope'.

4) bewildered
Both words mean 'confused'.

5) abundance
Both words mean 'more than enough'.

6) berserk
Both words mean 'crazy'.

7) flamboyant
Both words mean 'flashy'.

8) arbitrary
Both words mean 'with no pattern or reason'.

9) dismal
Both words mean 'dark and dreary'.

10) cheerful
Both words mean 'happy'.

11) frigid
Both words mean 'chilly'.

12) droll
Both words mean 'funny'.

13) introverted
Both words mean 'reserved'.

14) radiant
Both words mean 'emitting heat or light'.

15) condensed
Both words mean 'compressed'.

16) inventive
Both words mean 'imaginative'.

17) apathetic
Both words mean 'indifferent'.

18) congested
Both words mean 'clogged'.

Section 6: Numerical Reasoning

1) 100 000
When you add 1 to 99 999, the units column equals 10 so you carry the 1 into the next column. This continues through the number to give you 100 000.

2) 10
The difference between 31 and the starting number must be a multiple of 7: 31 − 10 = 21, which is 3 × 7. Alternatively, you could count back in 7s from 31 — 31, 24, 17, 10.

3) 7.04
The hundredths are the second column to the right of the decimal point. Look at the next decimal column to the right (the thousandths) to see whether to round up or down. Here there are 8 thousandths, so the number rounds up to 7.04.

4) 8
The number of lines of symmetry in a regular shape is equal to the number of sides. The eight lines of symmetry are shown below:

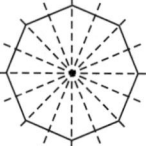

5) P, Q and S
A prism is a 3D shape that has the same face at each end. So there are three prisms: shapes P, Q and S. (A cube is a special prism, since all the edges are equal, but it is still a prism).

6) 6
2, 5 and 7 occur once; 3 and 4 occur twice; 6 occurs three times — so the dance club ordered more size 6 shoes.

7) 130 cm
The height of an average car is usually between 100 cm and 150 cm. 130 cm is the most likely figure as none of the other options are realistic.

8) 10
The key tells you that 1 symbol = 4 cars. There are 5 whole symbols for silver cars and $2\frac{1}{2}$ symbols for black cars. The difference between them is $5 - 2\frac{1}{2} = 2\frac{1}{2}$. Since $\frac{1}{2}$ a symbol shows $\frac{1}{2} \times 4 = 2$ cars, there are 8 + 2 = 10 more silver cars. Alternatively, find the difference in the number of cars. There are 5 symbols for silver cars. 5 symbols show 5 × 4 = 20 silver cars. There are $2\frac{1}{2}$ symbols for black cars. 2 symbols show 2 × 4 = 8 cars. $\frac{1}{2}$ a symbol shows $\frac{1}{2} \times 4 = 2$ cars. So there are 8 + 2 = 10 black cars. So the difference is 20 − 10 = 10.

9) 21
Work out how many people are left on the bus when 8 get off: 24 − 8 = 16 people.
5 people then got on the bus, so work out how many people are on the bus now: 16 + 5 = 21 people.

10) 480
Ignore the zero in the units column of each number and think of them as 21, 33, 34, 40 and 48. Then work out which of these numbers is in the 3 and 4 times table. The numbers that are in the 4 times table are 10 × 4 = 40 and 12 × 4 = 48. Of these two numbers only 48 is also divisible by 3 because the digits add up to a multiple of 3 (4 + 8 = 12).

11) 53°
Angles in a triangle add up to 180°. Add together the two known angles — 100° + 27° = 127°. Now subtract this from 180°. Missing angle x is 180° − 127° = 53°.

12) $\frac{1}{4}$
The cake is cut into 24 pieces. 18 of these are given away so there are 24 − 18 = 6 pieces left. As a fraction of the whole cake, this is $\frac{6}{24}$. The highest common factor of the numerator and denominator is 6, so divide the top and bottom by 6. This leads to 6 ÷ 6 = 1 and 24 ÷ 6 = 4, giving a fraction of $\frac{1}{4}$.

13) 3014
22 is half of 44, i.e. there are half as many erasers in one box as there are pencils. The answer to 137 × 22 must be half of the answer to 137 × 44. This is 6028 ÷ 2. You can work this out through partitioning: 6000 ÷ 2 = 3000, 28 ÷ 2 = 14, so the answer is 3014 erasers.

14) Wednesday
You could find all the Mondays by adding 7 each time: 4th June, 11th June, 18th June, 25th June. The 27th June is 2 days after the 25th June, so it is a Wednesday.

15) 72
To find the number that went into the machine you need to reverse the operations:
32 − 8 = 24
24 × 3 = 72.

16) −15 °C
If you count 9 down from −6 °C you get −15 °C.

17) £3.56
One method is to round both prices.
Add 1p to £4.99 to get £5 and 5p to £1.45 to get £1.50.
£5 + £1.50 = £6.50. Now take away the 6p extra you added.
£6.50 − 6p = £6.44.
The change from £10 is £10 − £6.44 = £3.56.

18) 252
10% of 560 is 56, so 5% of 560 is 28.
50% of 560 is 280.
45% of 560 is 50% − 5%, so 280 − 28 = 252.

19) (10, 7)
You need to find the x-coordinate first, then the y-coordinate. Look down from point B and read off the value on the x-axis (10). Then look across from B and read off the value on the y-axis (7). So the answer is (10, 7).

20) £3.10
Find the difference between the two amounts they have:
£21.60 − £15.40 = £6.20
Divide this by 2 to give you the amount Andrew should give to Julie: £6.20 ÷ 2 = £3.10

21) $2n + 15$
He saves £2 each week, so after n weeks he will have saved $2n$ pounds. He already had £15, so the total amount he will have is $2n + 15$.

22) 3 hours 5 minutes
The length of Jay's morning at school is 8.40 am until 12 noon which is 3 hours 20 minutes. Morning break is the only time Jay doesn't spend in lessons. This is 15 minutes long. So the time he spends in lessons is:
3 hours 20 minutes − 15 minutes = 3 hours 5 minutes.

23) 66
There are twice as many hard-centred chocolates as soft-centred ones, so there are 2 × 22 = 44 hard-centred chocolates. The total is 22 + 44 = 66.

Set A — Paper 2

Section 1: Verbal Reasoning — Cloze

1) rarest
'Giant pandas are the **rarest** bear species on the planet.'

2) native
'They are **native** to China'

3) considered
'they are **considered** to be a national treasure'

4) symbolise
'are often used to **symbolise** the country.'

5) reputation
'Their distinctive black and white markings and **reputation** for eating vast amounts of bamboo'

6) recognised
'they are **recognised** all over the world.'

7) like
'Giant pandas may look **like** massive teddy bears'

8) strength
'but their **strength** should not be underestimated.'

9) although
'Giant pandas have been known to attack humans, **although** rarely without provocation.'

10) destruction
'the **destruction** of the bamboo forests where they live'

11) only
'they are an endangered species, and **only** 1 600'

12) recorded
'1 600 were **recorded** as living in the wild in 2004.'

13) role
'pandas play an essential **role** in the forests where they reside.'

14) disperse
'They **disperse** seeds in their waste'

15) growth
'without these bears, the **growth** of the forest would suffer.'

16) preserve
'an attempt to **preserve** the giant panda and its habitat.'

Section 2: Numerical Reasoning

1 a) 140 m²
Calculate the whole area of the garden and then subtract the area of the patio. The area of a rectangle = length × width. The total area of the garden is 20 × 10 = 200 m² and the patio is 6 × 10 = 60 m².
So the lawn is 200 − 60 = 140 m².
Alternatively, break the shape of the lawn into separate rectangles and add their areas.

1 b) $\frac{1}{7}$
In part a), you found that the area of the lawn is 140 m². You can write 20 m² as a fraction of her lawn as $\frac{20}{140}$. The highest common factor of both 20 and 140 is 20.
So 20 ÷ 20 = 1 and 140 ÷ 20 = 7, leaving a fraction of $\frac{1}{7}$.

1 c) 24 m²
The area of the lawn left is 140 − 20 = 120 m². You can work out 10% of the area of the lawn by calculating 120 ÷ 10 = 12 m². 20% is 10% × 2, so 20% of 120 m² is 12 × 2 = 24 m².

2 a) 12
The key tells you that 1 symbol = 4 ladybirds. On Wednesday Robbie counted 14 ladybirds and on Thursday he counted 18.
14 + 18 = 32 ladybirds.
On Saturday Robbie counted 12 ladybirds and on Sunday he counted 8. 12 + 8 = 20 ladybirds.
So, 32 − 20 = 12 ladybirds.

2 b) 14
14 ladybirds (3$\frac{1}{2}$ ladybird symbols) were counted on both Wednesday and Friday.

2 c) 14
You need to add up the individual number of ladybirds found on each day, and divide this by the number of days in the week, 7.
22 + 10 + 14 + 18 + 14 + 12 + 8 = 98 ladybirds.
98 ÷ 7 = 14.

3 a) Lille and Paris
Read off the column and row which correspond to 224 km.

3 b) 353 km
Read off from the table how far away Tours and Calais are from Lille. Tours is 464 km away from Lille. Calais is 111 km away from Lille. Tours is 464 − 111 = 353 km further away than Calais from Lille.

3 c) 126 km
Read off from the graph the distance between Lille and Dijon, 504 km. Juliette travels $\frac{3}{4}$ of the distance on the first day. She travels $1 - \frac{3}{4} = \frac{1}{4}$ on the second day. $\frac{1}{4}$ of the total distance is 504 ÷ 4 = 126 km.

3 d) 5
The distance between Calais and Nice can be read off the table as 1258 km. You need to count up in steps of 250 km until you reach 1258 km or greater:
250, 500, 750, 1000, 1250, 1500. This is 6 steps, but by the sixth step he will have arrived in Calais, so you don't need to count that step as a fuel stop. So he stops for fuel 5 times.

4 a) £64
To find the next value in the pattern, double the last value.
So the 6th value is 32 × 2 = £64.

4 b) 24m − 10
The sequence goes up in steps of 24 each time. Therefore the expression involves 24m, where m is the month. The difference between the number generated from 24m and the actual value is 10, so the expression for the sequence is 24m − 10.

4 c) Karim
To work out how much Karim will have saved by the end of the 8th month, count up to the 8th term by doubling the previous term each month:
2, 4, 8, 16, 32, 64, 128, 256.
So after 8 months, Karim will have saved £256.
To find the amount of money Dave will have saved after 8 months, count up in steps of 24 from 14:
14, 38, 62, 86, 110, 134, 158, 182.
(Alternately you could use the expression in part 4 b), with m = 8 for the 8th month: 24 × 8 − 10 = £182.)
So Karim has saved more (£256) than Dave (£182) after 8 months.

5 a)   75
First you need to find the missing percentage.
22 + 28 + 35 = 85%. 100% − 85% = 15%.
So 15% of the plants sold were tulips.
Find 10% and 5% (as 10% + 5% = 15%):
10% of the number of plants sold is 500 ÷ 10 = 50.
5% of the number of plants sold is 50 ÷ 2 = 25.
The number of tulips sold is 50 + 25 = 75.

5 b)   140
First you need to work out how many roses were sold in total by finding 35% of 500.
You can work out 10% by calculating 500 ÷ 10 = 50.
5% is half of 10%, so 5% of 500 = 50 ÷ 2 = 25.
35% is 10% + 10% + 10% + 5%.
This is 50 + 50 + 50 + 25 = 175.
The ratio of red to white roses is 4:1. There are 4 + 1 = 5 shares in total. 1 share is equal to 175 ÷ 5 = 35. Red roses are worth 4 shares, so 35 × 4 = 140 red roses were sold.

5 c)   £630
First you need to calculate how many pansies were sold by calculating 28% of 500.
10% is 50, 5% is 25, and 1% is 5 plants.
28% = 10% + 10% + 5% + 1% + 1% + 1%.
This is 50 + 50 + 25 + 5 + 5 + 5 = 140 pansies.
Pansies sell for £4.50 each. The total value of the pansies sold is 4.5 × 140. This can be done through partitioning.
140 = 100 + 40.
4.5 × 100 = 450, 4.5 × 40 = 180, 450 + 180 = £630.

6 a)   Zebra Feeding
You need to work out how long each event lasts:
Penguin Feeding = 30 minutes
Big Cat Talk = 35 minutes
Gorilla Feeding = 25 minutes
Zebra Feeding = 20 minutes
Camel Rides = 55 minutes

6 b)   75 minutes
The African Adventure is 1 hour 40 minutes long. This is equal to 60 + 40 = 100 minutes.
The Gorilla Feeding is 25 minutes.
The African Adventure is therefore
100 − 25 = 75 minutes longer than the Gorilla Feeding.

6 c)   Lunch with Lions
The first tour after Jane arrives starts at 13:30 (there is a break for lunch from 11:55 - 13:30). The afternoon tours last 15 minutes so Jane will finish the tour at 13:45. This is 5 minutes before the Lunch with Lions finishes.

6 d)   45 minutes
The Big Cat Talk finishes at 12:45. There is a pause in tours between 11:55 and 1:30 pm. The first tour she can go on is at 1:30 pm. This is a wait of 45 minutes.

7 a)   A
The pieces fit into the puzzle as follows:

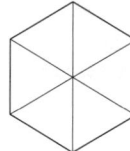

This creates 6 identical equilateral triangles. A is the only shape that is an equilateral triangle which will fit into the frame with no overlap, filling all the space.

7 b)   6
The lines of symmetry for a regular hexagon are shown below:

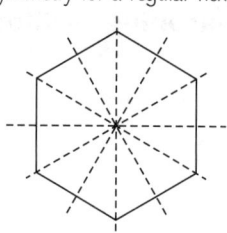

7 c)   C
The shapes are made with the two puzzle pieces. The shape in C requires the upper shape to be flipped/reflected in order to generate the shape. The others can be made through simple translation and/or rotation.

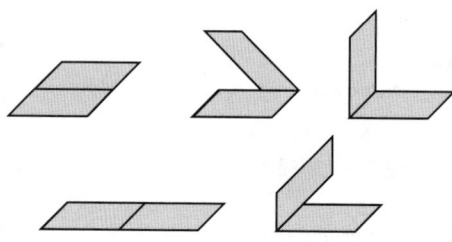

8 a)   (−2, 8)
When reading off coordinates, remember to give the value of the x-axis before the value of the y-axis.

8 b)   Bird House
The route Pranav took is shown on the map below.

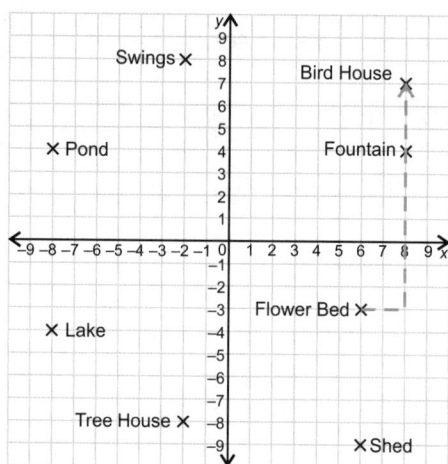

8 c) **Lake**

Pranav walks 6 metres south to arrive at point (−2, 2). From this point he turns to face south west. He will be able to see everything that lies on the dotted line, which includes the lake. The route Pranav took is shown on the map below.

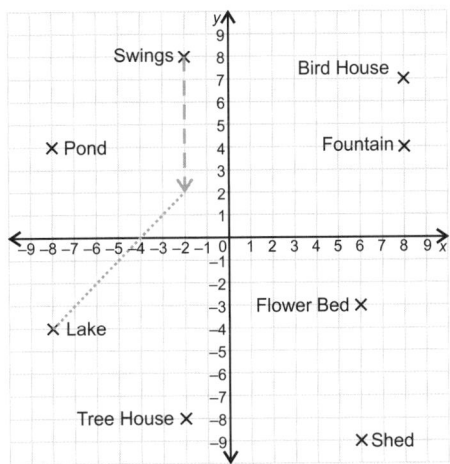

8 d) **Lake**

The x-axis is the axis that runs horizontally across the grid. The coordinates of the pond can be read off as (−8, 4). A reflection in the x-axis changes the sign of the y-coordinate. So, the coordinates of the reflected point are (−8, −4). This point corresponds to the lake.

9 a) **£2.50**

The combined mass of Sania's parcel is 1.55 + 0.05 = 1.6 kg. You need to find this mass on the x-axis and read up vertically until you reach a line. The first line you reach is Speedydrop. To find the price, read across from this point to the y-axis. The cost to send a 1.6 kg parcel with Speedydrop is £2.50.

9 b) **£5.00**

Firstly, you need to work out the total mass of the parcel. This is 2.2 + 1.6 + 0.8 = 4.6 kg. You need to find this mass on the x-axis and read up vertically until you reach a line. The first line you reach is Parcelprince. To find the price, read across from this point to the y-axis. The cost to send a 4.6 kg parcel with Parcelprince is £5.00.

9 c) **£6.00**

You need to find the cost to send the individual parcels with both companies by reading the masses and prices from the graph.
A 0.8 kg parcel costs £2.50 to send with Parcelprince.
A 3.2 kg parcel costs £4.00 to send with Parcelprince.
The total cost of sending both parcels with Parcelprince is £2.50 + £4.00 = £6.50.
A 0.8 kg parcel costs £1.50 to send with Speedydrop.
A 3.2 kg parcel costs £4.50 to send with Speedydrop.
The total cost of sending both parcels with Speedydrop is £1.50 + £4.50 = £6.00.
So Speedydrop is cheaper.

Section 3: Non-Verbal Reasoning

1) **C**
The figure has been rotated 270 degrees clockwise (or 90 degrees anticlockwise). Option A is a rotated reflection. Options B and D are different spirals.

2) **B**
The figure has been rotated 180 degrees. Option A is a reflection. In options C and D, the circles have the wrong shadings.

3) **A**
The figure has been rotated 90 degrees clockwise. Options B and C are different shapes. Option D is a rotated reflection.

4) **C**
The figure has been rotated 225 degrees clockwise (or 135 degrees anticlockwise). In option A, the triangle is the wrong way round. In option B, the hexagon is the wrong way round. In option D, both the triangle and the hexagon are the wrong way round.

5) **D**
The figure has been rotated 90 degrees clockwise. Option A is a reflection. Option B has the wrong arrowhead. Option C is a rotated reflection.

6) **A**
The figure has been rotated 225 degrees clockwise (or 135 degrees anticlockwise). Option B is a different shape. Option C has the wrong hatching. Option D is a rotated reflection.

7) **D**
The figure has been rotated 270 degrees clockwise (or 90 degrees anticlockwise). In options A and B, the three shapes are layered in the wrong order. In option C, the pentagon and the square have swapped shadings.

8) **B**
The figure has been rotated 90 degrees clockwise. In option A, the arrows are not pointing towards the centre of the cross and one is positioned incorrectly. In options C and D, the arrows are in the wrong 'arms' of the cross shape.

9) **B**
Working from left to right, the black circle moves diagonally down to the right in each grid square.

10) **C**
Working from right to left, the longest line disappears in each grid square.

11) **B**
Working from top to bottom, the top two grid squares are added together to make the bottom grid square.

12) **A**
The large shape is the same in all grid squares along each row. In each row, one grid square contains the large shape on its own, shaded white, one grid has a black inner shape and a white outer shape, and one grid square has a white inner shape and a black outer shape.

13) **A**
Working from left to right, the whole grid square rotates 90 degrees clockwise.

14) **A**
The three different grid squares (black ellipse in the centre, white ellipse in the top right-hand corner and white ellipse in the bottom left-hand corner) each appears once in each row and column.

15) **A**
Each direction that the arrow points in only appears once in each row and column. Each different type of arrowhead also only appears once in each row and column.

16) B
Along each row and down each column, the shape in the first grid square is added to the shape in the third grid square to make the shape in the second grid square.

17) E
All other figures have a smaller shape which is a 180 degree rotation of the larger shape. (E has a pentagon inside a hexagon.)

18) A
In all other figures, the arrow and the dot have different shadings.

19) E
All other figures are identical apart from rotation.

20) A
All other figures have four lines inside the shield shape.

21) E
In all other figures, the cross shape is on a corner.

22) E
In all other figures, the small black shape created by the overlap of the two large shapes has four sides.

23) B
The series alternates between a large square and a small triangle, and a large triangle and a small square.

24) A
The small inside shape gets bigger to become the large shape in the next series square and a new small shape appears inside it. (A is the only option where the large shape is a square with a dotted line.)

25) D
In each series square an extra line is added in an alternating pattern of a diagonal line and then a vertical line. The dot moves one place to the right and alternates colours between black and white.

26) C
Apart from the shadings, the entire figure rotates 90 degrees clockwise in each series square. The shading of the top left shape alternates between black and grey.

27) B
In each series square, the arrow rotates 180 degrees. The circle moves left along the top of the curved line.

28) B
In each series square, the inner shape rotates 90 degrees clockwise. The outer shape rotates 90 degrees anticlockwise.

29) D
Option A has not been reflected and it has the wrong shading. Option B has not been reflected and the black shape has been rotated. In option C, the shading is wrong.

30) B
Option A has been reflected across and downwards. In options C and D, the white arrow is pointing the wrong way.

31) C
Option A has been reflected downwards and rotated. Options B and D are the wrong shape.

32) B
In option A, the triangle has moved to the front. In option C, the triangle and the star have swapped positions and the triangle has moved to the front. In option D, the shapes at the front have moved to the back and the shapes at the back have moved to the front. The circle also has the wrong shading.

33) A
Option B has the wrong number of arrows. Option C has the wrong arrows. In option D, the arrows are in the wrong place.

34) D
In option A, the black square is in the wrong place. Option B has the wrong hatching. Option C has two black squares and the wrong hatching.

Set B — Paper 1

Section 1: Verbal Reasoning — Comprehension: an extract from 'Oliver Twist'

1) C
In the passage it says that Oliver kept hiding, "fearing that he might be pursued" — he expects someone to be coming after him.

2) C
Oliver thinks of London as "that great place!", and it is the possibility of going to London that makes him keep going — he "jumped upon his feet".

3) D
When Oliver is considering going to London, his first thought is that "nobody — not even Mr. Bumble — could ever find him there!". His main aim is to stay away from Mr Bumble.

4. A
Oliver has "a crust of bread, a coarse shirt, and two pairs of stockings, in his bundle", but the penny is "in his pocket".

5) A
"to no purpose" means 'with no results', so after all of his thinking about "how much he must undergo...to reach his place of destination", he still doesn't know how he will get to London.

6) C
In the passage, it says that the penny was "a gift of Sowerberry's" because Oliver had "acquitted himself more than ordinarily well" at a funeral. This means that he earned the money.

7) B
In the passage it says "He felt frightened at first, for the wind moaned dismally".

8) D
The passage says that "Oliver walked twenty miles that [first] day" and on the second day "he had walked no more than twelve miles, when night closed in again", so after the first two days Oliver had walked a total of 32 miles.

9) A
The text says that Oliver "tried to keep up with the coach" but was "unable". This means he couldn't run fast enough.

10) A
The passage mentions warning signs stating that all beggars "would be sent to jail".

11) A
In the passage it says that generally the landladies had Oliver sent away as they were "sure he had come to steal something". This shows that they were suspicious of him.

12) D
The passage says that Oliver has "a few draughts of water, which he begged at the cottage-doors" — the people living in the cottages are the only ones who help him.

13) C
Oliver is thinking about the "difficulties" that he faces and decides that his possessions aren't very useful things for such a long walk in wintertime.

14) C
Oliver realises "how much he must undergo" to get to London, and it is when the scale of his journey becomes clear that he begins to slow down.

15) B
Oliver ran after the coach when he was already tired and hungry, so by the time it leaves he must be exhausted.

16) A
"diminished" means 'reduced'. Oliver has walked further, so he has decreased the distance he must walk.

17) C
"surmounting" means 'overcoming'. Oliver can't think of a way to overcome his problems.

18) D
In this context, "obliged" means 'forced'. Oliver had no choice but to buy some food.

19) B
"awakened a new train of ideas" means 'made him think of a new plan'. The sign to London gives Oliver the idea to go to London.

20) D
"brought Oliver's heart into his mouth" means 'made Oliver frightened'. Oliver is afraid that he will be sent to a workhouse or orphanage.

Section 2: Verbal Reasoning — Cloze

1) Atlantic
'The Bermuda Triangle, or Devil's Triangle, is an area of the **Atlantic** Ocean'

2) location
'There is no formal **location** for the triangle'

3) official
'it can't be found on any **official** maps.'

4) alleged
'However, many ships and aircraft are **alleged** to have gone missing'

5) bizarre
'numerous sailors have had **bizarre** experiences'

6) between
'in the triangle of ocean **between** Miami, Puerto Rico and Bermuda.'

7) known
'Bermuda itself was once **known** as the 'Isle of Devils''

8) threat
'large areas of reefs which surround the island were a serious **threat** to boats'

9) shores
'sailed too close to its **shores**.'

10) peculiar
'One of the most **peculiar** incidents in the history of the Bermuda Triangle'

11) planes
'the disappearance of five bomber **planes** from 'Flight 19' in 1945.'

12) naval
'five aircraft left a **naval** base in Florida'

13) variety
'a **variety** of strange theories'

14) theories
'strange **theories** have been suggested'

15) years
'theories have been suggested over the **years**'

16) rational
'Some people have attempted to find **rational** explanations'

17) believe
'others prefer to **believe** that strange energy fields'

18) caused
'supernatural factors have **caused** the large number of unusual occurrences.'

19) unusual
'the large number of **unusual** occurrences.'

20) deny
'no one can **deny** that the mysterious tales'

21) curious
'one of the most **curious** stretches of water on the planet.'

Section 3: Verbal Reasoning — Odd One Out

1) draft
The other three are ways of displaying data.

2) ripe
The other three mean 'get bigger'.

3) wistful
The other three mean 'happy'.

4) disconnect
The other three mean 'combine'.

5) novel
The other three are reference books.

6) granite
The other three are types of metal.

7) shake
The other three involve using a utensil to create a mixture.

8) crimson
The other three are shades of purple.

9) hornet
The other three are insects that don't sting.

10) seam
The other three are all types of fastening that can be opened.

11) classroom
The other three rooms can be found in a house.

12) receive
The other three mean 'appeal for something'.

13) complicated
The other three mean 'visually unclear'.

14) rose
The other three are types of tree.

15) cube
The other three are two-dimensional shapes.

16) father
The other three are female relatives.

17) grin
The other three are facial expressions that show negative feelings.

18) dishevelled
The other three mean 'ungraceful'.

Section 4: Verbal Reasoning — Antonyms

1) pessimistic
'upbeat' means 'positive', whereas 'pessimistic' means 'negative'.

2) superficial
'significant' means 'important', whereas 'superficial' means 'not important'.

3) comprehensive
'limited' means 'restricted', whereas 'comprehensive' means 'complete'.

4) neglect
'maintain' means 'care for', whereas 'neglect' means 'ignore'.

5) humble
'conceited' means 'arrogant', whereas 'humble' means 'modest'.

6) disturbed
'tranquil' means 'calm', whereas 'disturbed' means 'disrupted'.

7) magnanimous
'selfish' means 'thinking of oneself', whereas 'magnanimous' means 'generous to others'.

8) reasonable
'stubborn' means 'not prepared to compromise', whereas 'reasonable' means 'prepared to compromise'.

9) disapproval
'acceptance' means 'agreement', whereas 'disapproval' means 'refusal to agree'.

10) perplexing
'clear' means 'obvious', whereas 'perplexing' means 'confusing'.

11) reserved
'assured' means 'confident', whereas 'reserved' means 'shy'.

12) lethargic
'lively' means 'energetic', whereas 'lethargic' means 'lacking energy'.

13) daring
'cowardly' means 'fearful', whereas 'daring' means 'brave'.

14) composed
'nervous' means 'anxious', whereas 'composed' means 'calm'.

15) withdraw
'contribute' means 'add', whereas 'withdraw' means 'take away'.

16) chaotic
'organised' means 'in order', whereas 'chaotic' means 'disorderly'.

17) bind
'detach' means 'separate', whereas 'bind' means 'join'.

18) superfluous
'necessary' means 'needed', whereas 'superfluous' means 'more than is needed'.

Section 5: Non-Verbal Reasoning

1) F
Shape F has been rotated 90 degrees left-to-right.

2) C
Shape C has been rotated 180 degrees in the plane of the page.

3) A
Shape A has been rotated 180 degrees left-to-right.

4) D
Shape D has been rotated 90 degrees left-to-right. Then it has been rotated 90 degrees away from you, top-to-bottom.

5) B
Shape B has been rotated 90 degrees towards you, top-to-bottom. Then it has been rotated 90 degrees left-to-right.

6) E
Shape E has been rotated 90 degrees left-to-right. Then it has been rotated 90 degrees towards you, top-to-bottom.

7) D
The top block of set D rotates 90 degrees left-to-right to become the left part of the figure on the left. The bottom block of the set moves to become the top right-hand part of the figure.

8) A
One of the top blocks of set A rotates 90 degrees clockwise in the plane of the page. The other top block of the set rotates 90 degrees towards you top-to-bottom and moves to the right of the first block to become the bottom right block of the figure. The bottom block moves to the back to become the top block of the figure.

9) C
The right-hand block of set C moves in front of the left-hand block to become the front left block of the figure. The top block of the set rotates 90 degrees left-to-right and moves down to become the bottom right-hand block of the figure.

10) B
The bottom left-hand block of set B rotates 90 degrees in the plane of the page to become the block at the back of the figure. The top block of the set rotates 90 degrees in the plane of the page, and then rotates 90 degrees away from you, top-to-bottom. It then moves to become the bottom front block in the figure. The bottom right block of the set rotates 90 degrees in the plane of the page and becomes the top block of the figure.

11) B
There should be four blocks visible from above, which rules out options A, C and D.

12) A
There should be four blocks visible from above, which rules out options B and D. There are two blocks visible at the front of the figure, which rules out option C.

13) C
There should be five blocks visible from above, which rules out options A and D. There is a row of three blocks at the front of the figure, which rules out option B.

14) D
There are three blocks visible at the front of the figure, which rules out option A and B. There are four blocks visible on the right hand side which rules out C.

15) A
Option B is ruled out because if the face with the black stripe was on the top and the face with the triangle was at the front, the circle on the right-hand face would be black, not white. Options C and D are ruled out because they contain shapes that don't appear on the net (option C has a white rectangle and option D has a grey triangle).

16) B
Option A is ruled out because the black square and the letter 'Y' should be on opposite sides. Option C is ruled out because there is only one grey triangle on the net. Option D is ruled out because the letter 'Y' has the wrong rotation.

17) D
Option A is ruled out because the black circle and the three diagonal lines should be on opposite sides of the cube. Option B is ruled out because if the star was on the top and the circle was at the front, the face on the right would be the black stripe. Option C is ruled out because the black stripe and the diagonal lines have the wrong rotation.

18) D
Option A is ruled out because the white circle and the black L-shape should be on opposite sides. Option B is ruled out because there is no white arrow on the net. Option C is ruled out because one of the arrowheads should be pointing at the black L-shape.

Set B — Paper 2

Section 1: Numerical Reasoning

1 a) 42
Jamila picked $3\frac{1}{2}$ punnets of apples. Each punnet contains 12 apples. You need to work out $3\frac{1}{2} \times 12$.
You can do this using partitioning.
$3 \times 12 = 36$. $\frac{1}{2} \times 12$ is equivalent to $12 \div 2 = 6$.
The total number of apples picked is $36 + 6 = 42$.

1 b) 21
Jamila picked 4 punnets of pears. This is equivalent to $4 \times 12 = 48$ pears. Jamila picked $2\frac{1}{4}$ punnets of plums. You need to work out $2\frac{1}{4} \times 12$. You can do this using partitioning. $2 \times 12 = 24$. $\frac{1}{4} \times 12$ is equivalent to $12 \div 4 = 3$. The total number of plums picked is $24 + 3 = 27$. Jamila picked $48 - 27 = 21$ more pears than plums.

1 c) 8:7
You have already calculated how many pears and apples Jamila picked. She picked 48 pears and 42 apples.
As a ratio, this is 48:42.
The highest common factor of both 48 and 42 is 6.
$48 \div 6 = 8$. $42 \div 6 = 7$. This gives the ratio of pears:apples as 8:7.
Alternatively you could express the ratio in terms of the number of punnets. Jamila picked 4 punnets of pears and $3\frac{1}{2}$ punnets of apples. As a ratio this is $4:3\frac{1}{2}$. You need to multiply both sides by 2 to get only whole numbers.
$4 \times 2 = 8$. $3\frac{1}{2} \times 2 = 7$.
This is a ratio of 8:7.

1 d) £5.00
The price of $\frac{1}{4}$ punnet of plums is 60p. So to work out the price of a full punnet you need to multiply that price by 4.
$60 \times 4 = 240$p.
There's a 20p discount for every full punnet, so each full punnet costs $240p - 20p = 220p$
Jamila picked 2 whole punnets of plums, plus another $\frac{1}{4}$ punnet.
So the total cost will be:
$220p + 220p + 60p = 500p = £5.00$

2 a) $\frac{7}{51}$
Derren removes the King of Diamonds. This means the number of Queens or Kings in the pack has decreased by 1. To start with there were 8 Queens and Kings in the pack altogether. There are $8 - 1 = 7$ remaining. The number of cards in the pack has also decreased by 1. There are now $52 - 1 = 51$ cards in the pack. This gives a fraction of $\frac{7}{51}$.

2 b) $\frac{22}{47}$
The number of cards that have been taken out of the pack has decreased by 5, giving $52 - 5 = 47$ cards left. The number of red cards has only decreased by 4. There were 26 red cards to start off with, so the number remaining in the pack is $26 - 4 = 22$. This gives a fraction of $\frac{22}{47}$.

2 c) 2
If Derren removes 12 cards from the pack, he will have $52 - 12 = 40$ cards remaining. $\frac{1}{20}$ of 40 is equivalent to $40 \div 20 = 2$. This means there are 2 aces left in the pack. There are 4 aces in a whole pack of cards, so $4 - 2 = 2$ must have been removed in the 12 cards.

3 a) 160 000 cm³
The volume of the tank is equal to width × height × depth. You need to calculate $80 \times 50 \times 40$. $80 \times 50 = 4000$. You then need to work out $4000 \times 40 = 160\ 000$ cm³.

3 b) 120 000 cm³
$\frac{1}{4}$ of the tank is 160 000 cm³ $\div$ 4.
Start by imagining the calculation without the 0s:
$16 \div 4 = 4$, so $160\ 000 \div 4 = 40\ 000$ cm³.
$\frac{1}{4}$ of 160 000 cm³ is 40 000 cm³, so $\frac{3}{4}$ of 160000 cm³ is $3 \times 40\ 000 = 120\ 000$ cm³.

3 c) 120 litres
You need to work out $120000 \div 1000$. To divide by 1000, you need to move the digits 3 places to the right.
$120000 \div 1000 = 120$ litres.

3 d) 12
For every 10 litres, Kim can keep 1 fish. You need to work out how many lots of 10 litres there are in 120 litres. You can do this by doing $120 \div 10$. To divide by 10, move the digits one place to the right. $120 \div 10 = 12$. So Kim can keep 12 fish in the tank.

4 a)   (3, 7)
Ben moves clockwise at 2 metres a second. If he runs for 10 seconds he will cover 10 × 2 = 20 squares. Ben's journey looks like this, and he will end up at (3, 7).

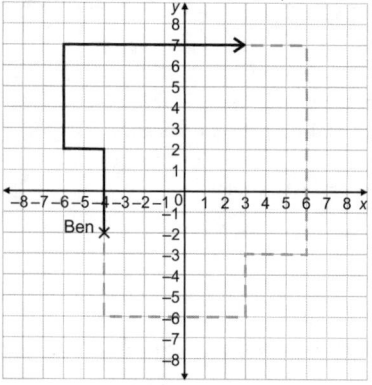

4 b)   (6, 1)
Emma starts running towards Abu. By the time Abu starts running Emma has already covered 3 metres, or 3 squares. Their journey will look like this:

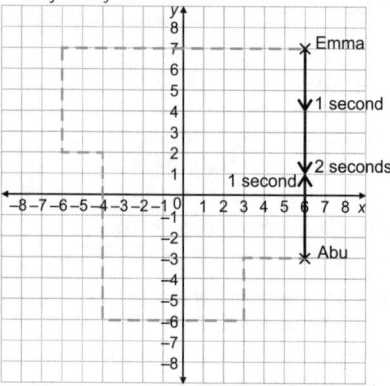

Abu and Emma will arrive at point (6, 1) at the same time.

4 c)   (3, –4)
Alice runs at 6 metres per second. Caley runs at 0.5 metres per second. This means Caley only covers half a square in the time it takes for Alice to cover 6. Alice will catch up with Caley at (3, –4):

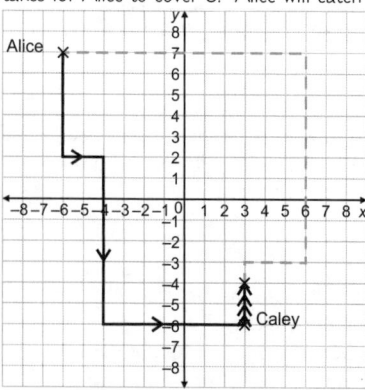

5 a)   30°
The corner of a rectangle is 90°. Angle x is equal to 90 – 60 = 30°.

5 b)   80°
Angles in a triangle add up to 180°. 60 + 40 + y = 180°. You need to work out 180 – 60 – 40. 60 + 40 = 100, so 180 – 100 = 80°.

5 c)   Scalene
The triangle marked A has 3 different angles and 3 different length sides. It is a scalene triangle.

5 d)   130°
Angles in a quadrilateral add up to 360°. The shape has 2 right angles of 90°. It has two unknown angles. The first unknown angle can be calculated as 90 – 40 = 50°, using the angle from the triangle.
This means angle z must be equal to 360 – 90 – 90 – 50. 90 + 90 + 50 = 230, so z = 360 – 230 = 130°.

6 a)   1800 cm²
You need to work out the area of the overall frame and then subtract the area of the picture. The area of the whole frame is 120 × 40 = 4800 cm². The area of the picture centre is 100 × 30 = 3000 cm². The area of the border is the difference between these two numbers.
4800 – 3000 = 1800 cm².

6 b)   100
You need to work out how many photos you can fit along the length of the picture space. One photo is 5 cm wide. To work out how many you can fit in one row, you need to calculate 100 ÷ 5 = 20 photos. To work out how many rows of 20 photos you fit in the height of the picture space, you need to calculate 30 ÷ 6 = 5 rows. 5 rows of 20 photos is equivalent to 20 × 5 = 100 photos in total.

6 c)   1200 cm²
The area of one photo is 5 × 6 = 30 cm². The area occupied by 40 photos is 30 × 40 = 1200 cm².

6 d)   525 cm²
The area of the picture space of the smaller frame was calculated in part c. The area of the border is equal to the area of the picture space subtracted from the overall area.
1725 – 1200 = 525 cm².

7 a)   39
Each music note symbol represents 6 children. There are 6 full symbols and one half symbol in the row for piano. This is equal to (6 × 6) + (6 ÷ 2). 6 × 6 = 36. 6 ÷ 2 = 3. The total number of children that said the piano was their favourite instrument is 36 + 3 = 39.

7 b)   12
There are 3½ symbols for the guitar. This is equal to (3 × 6) + (6 ÷ 2): 3 × 6 = 18. 6 ÷ 2 = 3. 18 + 3 = 21 children preferred guitar.
There are 1½ symbols for the flute. This is equal to 6 + (6 ÷ 2) = 6 + 3 = 9 children. The number of children who preferred the guitar to the flute is 21 – 9 = 12.

7 c)   30
9 children said the cello was their favourite instrument. 39 children said the piano was their favourite instrument. So there were 39 – 3 = 30 fewer children who said cello than piano.

7 d)   Cello, Flute and Guitar
You can answer this question by counting up the number of symbols that each category has:
Piano: 6½
Flute: 1½
Cello: 1½
Drums: 3
Guitar: 3½
You need to find a combination that adds up to 6½. The cello, the flute and the guitar combined are as popular as the piano:
1½ + 1½ + 3½ = 1 + 1 + 3 + ½ + ½ + ½ = 5 + 1½ = 6½.

8 a) 126 − 6*m*
The temperature of the cake decreases by 6 °C every minute. So the expression will involve −6*m*. The only expression that includes this is 126 − 6*m*. If you substitute in the values of *m* you can check that this expression is correct.

8 b) 60 °C
In part a) you worked out that the expression for the cooling of the cake was 126 − 6*m*. You can substitute the value of *m* = 11 into this expression to find the temperature after 11 minutes. 126 − (11 × 6) = 126 − 66 = 60 °C. Alternatively you can count down in steps of 6 from 120 until you reach the 11th term:
120, 114, 108, 102, 96, 90, 84, 78, 72, 66, 60.

8 c) 16 minutes
You need the temperature to be equal to 30 °C or lower.
126 − 6*m* = 30.
126 = 30 + 6*m*.
126 − 30 = 6*m*.
96 = 6*m*.
96 ÷ 6 = *m*. This can be done through partitioning. 90 splits into 60 + 36. 60 ÷ 6 = 10. 36 ÷ 6 = 6.
10 + 6 = 16. *m* = 16 minutes.
Alternately you can count down in steps of 6 from 120:
120, 114, 108, 102, 96, 90, 84, 78, 72, 66, 60, 54, 48, 42, 36, 30. 30 is the 16th term.

9 a) £65
You need to work out 90 × 1.5. You can do this using partitioning. 90 × 1 = £90. 90 × 0.5 is equivalent to 90 ÷ 2 = £45. The total money raised from selling the magazines is 90 + 45 = £135. The school paid £70 on printing, so the profit is 135 − 60 = £65.

9 b) 30
You need to work out 45 ÷ 1.5. You can do this by doubling both values so you are dealing with whole numbers.
45 × 2 = 90, 1.5 × 2 = 3,
so 45 ÷ 1.5 = 90 ÷ 3 = 30 children.

9 c) £54
The price of the school magazine increases by 20% so you need to work out 20% of £45.
10% of 45 is 45 ÷ 10 = 4.5.
20% is double this, so 20% = 4.5 × 2 = £9.
So the cost of the magazines for class A will be 45 + 9 = £54.

10 a) £28
You need to substitute the values for *d* and *m* into the equation for Canine Companions: 4(*d* + *m*).
Franz has 2 dogs and wants them to be walked 5 miles:
4 × (2 + 5) = 4 × 7 = £28.

10 b) £30
You need to substitute the values for *d* and *m* into the equation for Happy Tails: 5(*dm*) ÷ 2.
Ollie has 3 dogs and wants them to be walked 4 miles:
5(3 × 4) ÷ 2 = (5 × 12) ÷ 2 = 60 ÷ 2 = £30

10 c) Canine Companions
You need to substitute the values for *d* and *m* into the equations for all four companies and find the cheapest.
Xia owns 5 dogs and wants them walked 6 miles.
Pooch Pals: (10 × 5) + 6 = 50 + 6 = £56.
Barking Buddies: 2 × 5 × 6 = 10 × 6 = £60.
Canine Companions: 4(5 + 6) = 4 × 11 = £44.
Happy Tails: (5 × 5 × 6) ÷ 2 = (5 × 30) ÷ 2 = 150 ÷ 2 = £75.

10 d) 8 miles
You need to substitute the cost and the number of dogs into the equation for Pooch Pals:
58 = (10 × 5) + *m*.
58 = 50 + *m*.
58 − 50 = *m*.
8 = *m*.

11 a) 11:14
The buses run every half an hour. You need to take the time that the bus arrives in Sidton from the previous column and add 30 minutes. 10:44 + 30 minutes = 11:14.

11 b) 16 minutes
You need to work out the difference between the time the bus arrived in Halldon and the time the bus arrives in Plymstone. It arrives in Halldon at 11:43 and arrives in Plymstone at 11:59.
59 − 43 = 16 minutes later.

11 c) Halldon
72 minutes is equivalent to 60 + 12 minutes. This is 1 hour and 12 minutes. 1 hour after 11:01 is 12:01. 12 minutes on from 12:01 is 12:13. This is the time the bus arrives in Halldon.

11 d) 12:43
Firstly, you need to work out the total delay. The bus was delayed by 15 + 8 = 23 minutes. The bus is due to arrive in Ide at 12:20. It will arrive 23 minutes later, so the bus will arrive at 12:20 + 23 = 12:43.

12 a) 10 km
The furthest point away from the house was 5 km. Zhi ran 5 km out and 5 km home. His total run was 5 + 5 = 10 km.

12 b) 25 minutes
The points that Zhi is resting are shown by the parts of the graph where the line is flat. Zhi rests between 10 and 20 minutes, 35 and 45 minutes and 65 and 70 minutes. This is a total of: 10 + 10 + 5 = 25 minutes.

12 c) 0 - 10 minutes
The time at which Zhi is running the fastest is the time at which he covers the longest distance in the shortest time. It will be where the line on the graph is the steepest. This is at the start of the run between 0 and 10 minutes.

13 a) £4.70
Large milkshakes cost £3.50. Jake buys one standard topping (strawberries) for 20p extra. He also buys two deluxe toppings (fudge and blueberries) for 50p extra each. The total cost of the milkshake is £3.50 + 20p + 50p + 50p = £4.70.

13 b) 3
Medium milkshakes cost £3.00. If Katie spent £4.10 on a milkshake, she must have spent 4.10 − 3 = £1.10 on toppings. Standard toppings cost 20p. Katie can't spend exactly £1.10 just on standard toppings, so she must have bought at least 1 deluxe topping. If she bought 2 deluxe toppings (£1.00) she also couldn't have spent exactly £1.10.
She must have only bought 1 deluxe topping, leaving her with:
£1.10 − 50p = 60p to spend on standard toppings.
This is 60 ÷ 20 = 3 standard toppings.

13 c) £2.20
Milkshakes have a 20% discount on a Monday.
Small milkshakes usually cost £2.00. 10% of £2.00 is 20p, so 20% is equal to 20 × 2 = 40p. Small milkshakes will cost £2.00 − 40p = £1.60. Sadaf also gets 50% off toppings, so standard toppings will cost 20 ÷ 2 = 10p each and deluxe toppings will cost 50 ÷ 2 = 25p each.
Sadaf buys 1 standard topping and 2 deluxe toppings.
In total she will spend £1.60 + 10p + 25p + 25p = £2.20.

14 a) 49.5 acres
You need to work out what 11% of 450 acres is. You can start by calculating 10% which is 450 ÷ 10. To divide by 10, move the digits one place to the right.
10% of 450 = 45 acres. To work out 1% you need to do 450 ÷ 100. To divide by 100, move the digits two places to the right. 450 ÷ 100 = 4.5. 11% = 10% + 1%.
11% of 450 = 45 + 4.5 = 49.5 acres.

14 b) 63 acres
Start by finding $\frac{1}{50}$ of 450 acres: 450 ÷ 50 = 9 acres. Farmer Charles has assigned $\frac{7}{50}$ of 450 acres to wheat. So this is 7 × 9 = 63 acres.

14 c) 10%
You need to work out what 45 acres is as a percentage of 450. 450 ÷ 45 = 10, therefore 45 = 10% of the land.

14 d) Maize
You already know the percentage of land assigned for barley, cows and sheep. You calculated in part c that 10% of the land was assigned to maize. This is less than barley, cows or sheep. You know that wheat had an assignment of 63 acres. This is greater than the 45 acres which were assigned to maize.

Section 2: Verbal Reasoning — Cloze

1) take
'people all over the world *take* phones for granted.'

2) invented
'the first practical telephone wasn't *invented* until the late nineteenth century.'

3) patent
'Bell was awarded a *patent* for the telephone in 1876.'

4) different
'Bell's telephone was very *different* to those we use today.'

5) portable
'It was much bigger, and definitely not *portable*!'

6) research
'Bell's *research* on hearing, elocution and speech'

7) influenced
'was *influenced* by the fact that his mother and wife were both deaf.'

8) created
'before he *created* the telephone.'

9) on
'The first comprehensive sentence that Bell said *on* his telephone was "Mr Watson...come here...I want to see you."'

10) Within
'*Within* ten years, more than 150 000 people in America owned telephones'

11) his
'Bell refused to have a telephone in *his* own study'

12) productive
'he thought it would make him less *productive*.'

13) thought
'Although Bell *thought* his telephone would be a distraction'

14) essential
'most people regard phones as an *essential* part of everyday life.'

Section 3: Non-Verbal Reasoning

1) A
All figures are reflected across and the outline of the white shape swaps between solid and dashed.

2) C
All figures rotate 90 degrees clockwise. The shading of the head of the arrow-style line swaps between black and white.

3) C
All figures are reflected downwards and the two shapes in each figure swap shadings.

4) B
The shape at the top of the figure moves to the left of the new figure and the shape at the bottom of the figure moves to the right of the new figure. The left hand shape moves to the front and the right hand shape moves to the back.

5) C
The number of sides of the shape goes down by two, and two dots disappear.

6) B
The shapes in each figure move around one place anticlockwise. The shadings stay in their original positions.

7) D
Going in a clockwise direction from the top right-hand hexagon, the number of dots increases by one. The dots alternate between being at the top and the bottom of the hexagon.

8) D
The shapes are reflected across the middle of the hexagonal grid.

9) E
The pattern in each hexagon is reflected across the middle of the hexagonal grid.

10) B
Moving in a clockwise direction around the hexagonal grid, the thick white arrow rotates 60 degrees clockwise. The thin black arrow rotates 60 degrees anticlockwise.

11) C
Moving in a clockwise direction, the big, outside shape becomes the small, inside shape in the next hexagon and a new big shape appears.

12) B
All figures must be triangles with an arrow-style line pointing right.

13) D
All figures must have a circle as the outside shape.

14) A
In all figures, a small white arrow must point towards a black shape.

15) D
In all figures, the small grey shape must be the same as half of the large white shape but rotated.

16) D
In all figures, the middle shape must be identical to the shapes on the right and left, but rotated 180 degrees.

BLANK PAGE

11+ Practice Papers

For the **CEM** test

Answer Sheets

Ages 10-11

Pack 2

BLANK PAGE

Using the Multiple Choice Answer Sheets

If you're doing a Multiple Choice paper, it's often marked by a computer. These tests use special answer sheets like the ones in this booklet.

There's a Multiple Choice answer sheet to go with each Practice Paper, so make sure you're filling in the right one. If you get used to these answer sheets now, it means there'll be no nasty surprises when you sit the real test.

Here are a few tips for using the answer sheets without getting yourself in a pickle...

Tips for Filling in the Answer Sheets

1) Before you start, fill in your name and the name of your school in the correct space. There may be boxes for other information, like your date of birth or your pupil number. Make sure you don't leave anything blank by mistake.

2) To mark your answer, put a clear pencil line through the answer box.

3) Make sure you have a pencil sharpener and an eraser for any mistakes.

4) If you make a mistake, rub out the incorrect answer first, and then fill in your new answer clearly.

5) It's easy to lose your place when you move from the test paper to the answer sheet, so match up the question number on the paper and the answer sheet. Keeping the two sheets close together will help you do this.

6) If you skip a question to come back to later, make sure you leave a gap for that question on the answer sheet. That way your answers will stay in order.

7) Don't do rough working on your answer sheet.

8) Don't worry if you mark boxes in the same position several times in a row — just because you've marked the second box four times, it doesn't mean that your answers are wrong.

Set A: Paper 1

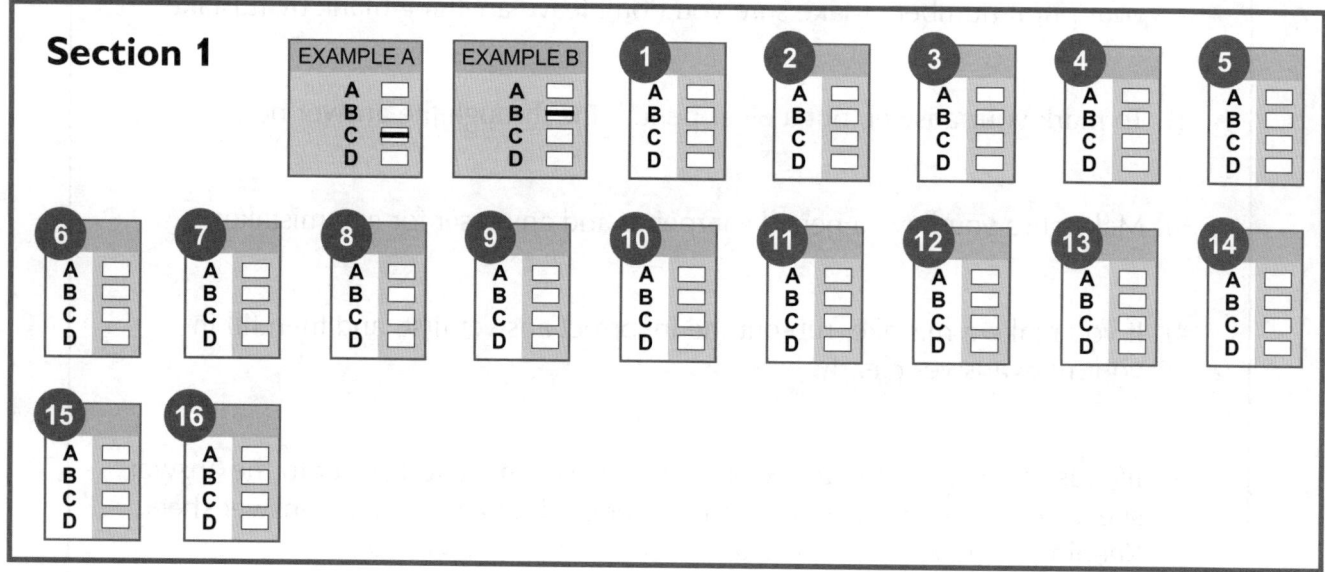

Section 3

EXAMPLE
freckle ☐
smudge ☐
spot ■
see ☐

1
store ☐
bank ☐
bay ☐
secure ☐

2
back ☐
endorse ☐
tail ☐
end ☐

3
ability ☐
jar ☐
bottle ☐
can ☐

4
money ☐
adapt ☐
change ☐
excess ☐

5
obvious ☐
free ☐
release ☐
clear ☐

6
fair ☐
just ☐
light ☐
honourable ☐

7
tight ☐
grasp ☐
purchase ☐
trade ☐

8
full ☐
matched ☐
bound ☐
engaged ☐

9
garden ☐
plant ☐
mill ☐
yard ☐

10
light ☐
shiny ☐
upbeat ☐
chirpy ☐

11
confer ☐
converse ☐
contrary ☐
gossip ☐

12
charter ☐
pass ☐
authorise ☐
permit ☐

Section 4

Each word has two or more missing letters. Mark the box next to each letter that needs to be added to complete the word.

EXAMPLE
? e ? k
s ☐ w ■ p ☐ | a ■ e ☐ i ☐

1 t ? i ? ? a l
h ☐ r ☐ o ☐ | v ☐ g ☐ t ☐ | e ☐ i ☐ u ☐

2 c ? ? t i o ? s
o ☐ u ☐ a ☐ | u ☐ a ☐ r ☐ | u ☐ a ☐ s ☐

3 w ? ? l ? l y
h ☐ r ☐ o ☐ | r ☐ o ☐ t ☐ | i ☐ d ☐ b ☐

4 f ? i ? ? l o u s
e ☐ r ☐ l ☐ | u ☐ c ☐ v ☐ | u ☐ o ☐ a ☐

5 f ? a ? l
r ☐ e ☐ l ☐ | i ☐ u ☐ e ☐

6 ? ? e
d ☐ s ☐ f ☐ | o ☐ e ☐ u ☐

7 p r ? v ? n
o ☐ a ☐ u ☐ | a ☐ e ☐ i ☐

8 p ? o f o ? ? d
l ☐ r ☐ h ☐ | u ☐ a ☐ o ☐ | l ☐ m ☐ n ☐

9 m ? b i ? ?
o ☐ a ☐ u ☐ | r ☐ a ☐ l ☐ | e ☐ y ☐ l ☐

10 ? a ? i ? d
c ☐ v ☐ h ☐ | r ☐ t ☐ s ☐ | e ☐ a ☐ o ☐

11 q u ? r ? ?
i ☐ e ☐ a ☐ | c ☐ t ☐ k ☐ | e ☐ y ☐ i ☐

12 f l ? ? p ? n t
i ☐ a ☐ e ☐ | m ☐ p ☐ s ☐ | a ☐ e ☐ i ☐

13 p ? s ? i ? e
i ☐ a ☐ u ☐ | t ☐ s ☐ h ☐ | v ☐ t ☐ c ☐

14 ? r ? u o ? s
t ☐ a ☐ e ☐ | d ☐ t ☐ a ☐ | i ☐ u ☐ l ☐

15 l ? ? t ? r
e ☐ a ☐ o ☐ | i ☐ o ☐ s ☐ | e ☐ a ☐ u ☐

16 ? o ? f ? i t
c ☐ s ☐ f ☐ | r ☐ l ☐ m ☐ | e ☐ a ☐ u ☐

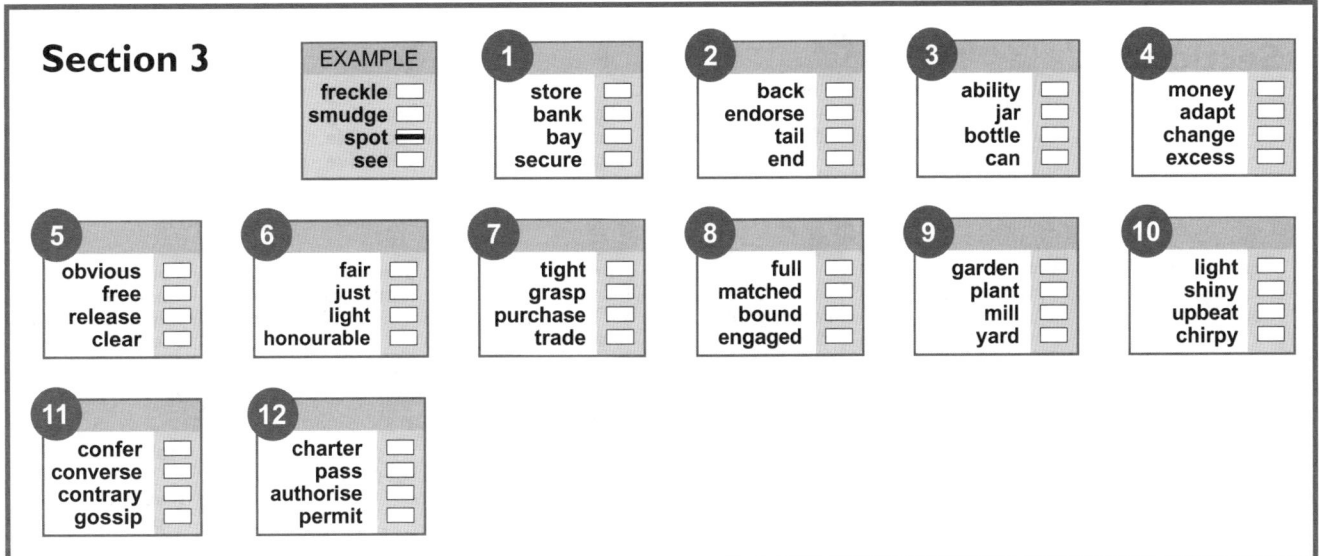

Section 5

EXAMPLE
- tiny
- strong
- large
- soft

1
- decline
- renounce
- despise
- revere

2
- dark
- blighted
- austere
- gaunt

3
- promising
- interesting
- impossible
- selective

4
- excited
- blinded
- gleeful
- bewildered

5
- generous
- full
- abundance
- deficit

6
- enthusiastic
- disturbed
- delirious
- berserk

7
- rare
- expensive
- flamboyant
- decorative

8
- irrelevant
- casual
- lucky
- arbitrary

9
- atmospheric
- monotonous
- ambient
- dismal

10
- morose
- melodic
- cheerful
- energetic

11
- frigid
- shiver
- passive
- temperate

12
- absurd
- droll
- clown
- quizzical

13
- gregarious
- abrupt
- introverted
- restrained

14
- radiant
- pallid
- opaque
- blazing

15
- crowded
- condensed
- foldable
- useful

16
- talented
- artist
- inventive
- prolific

17
- enthusiastic
- idle
- apathetic
- stolid

18
- congested
- busy
- crowded
- obstruction

Section 6

EXAMPLE A
- $^3/_4$
- $^1/_2$
- $^{10}/_{16}$
- $^{18}/_{36}$
- $^1/_5$

EXAMPLE B

£ 1 7 . 9 4

0 1 2 3 4 5 6 7 8 9

1

miles

0 1 2 3 4 5 6 7 8 9

2
- 2
- 5
- 7
- 10
- 16

3

.

0 1 2 3 4 5 6 7 8 9

4

0 1 2 3 4 5 6 7 8 9

5
- P, Q and S
- Q, R and T
- P and S only
- R and T only
- Only S

6

0 1 2 3 4 5 6 7 8 9

7
- 13 m
- 1.3 km
- 130 cm
- 130 mm
- 13 cm

8

0 1 2 3 4 5 6 7 8 9

9

0 1 2 3 4 5 6 7 8 9

10
- 210
- 330
- 340
- 400
- 480

11

°

0 1 2 3 4 5 6 7 8 9

12
- $^3/_4$
- $^2/_9$
- $^1/_3$
- $^4/_9$
- $^1/_4$

13

0 1 2 3 4 5 6 7 8 9

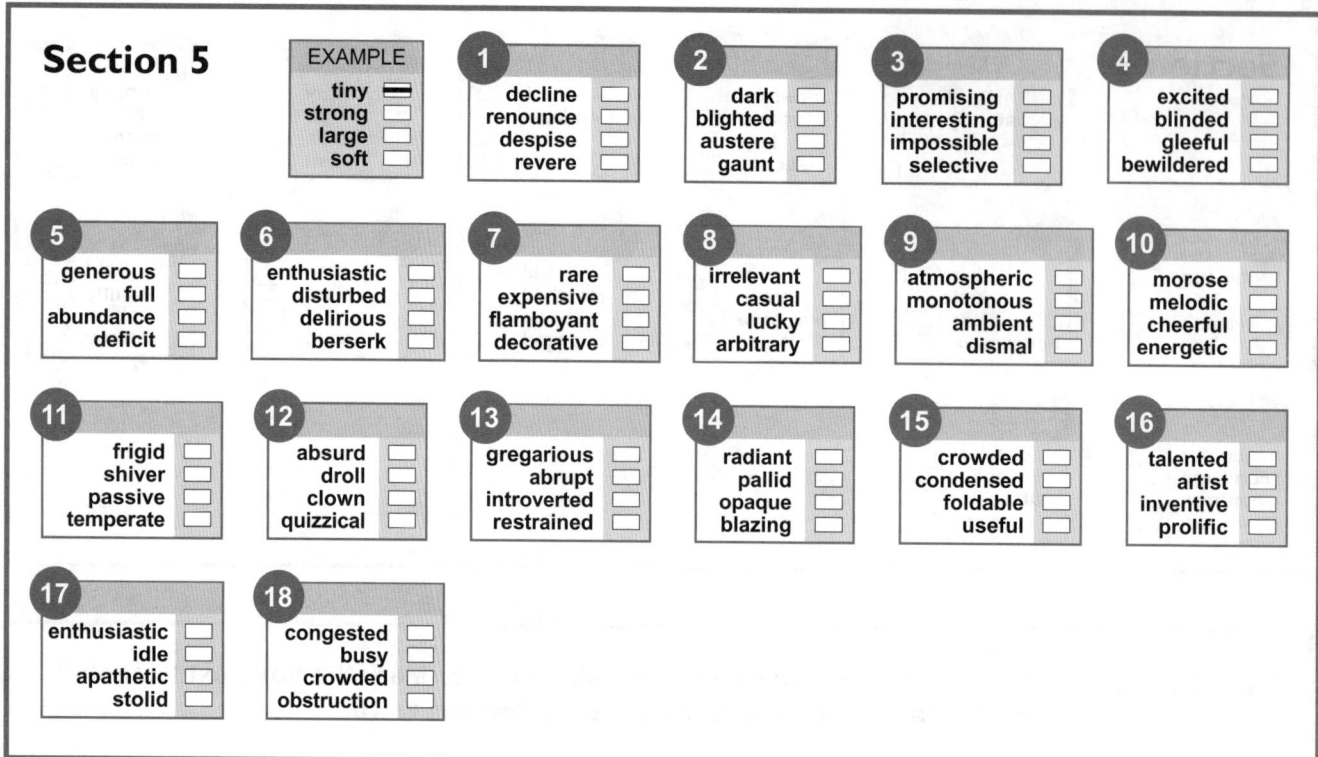

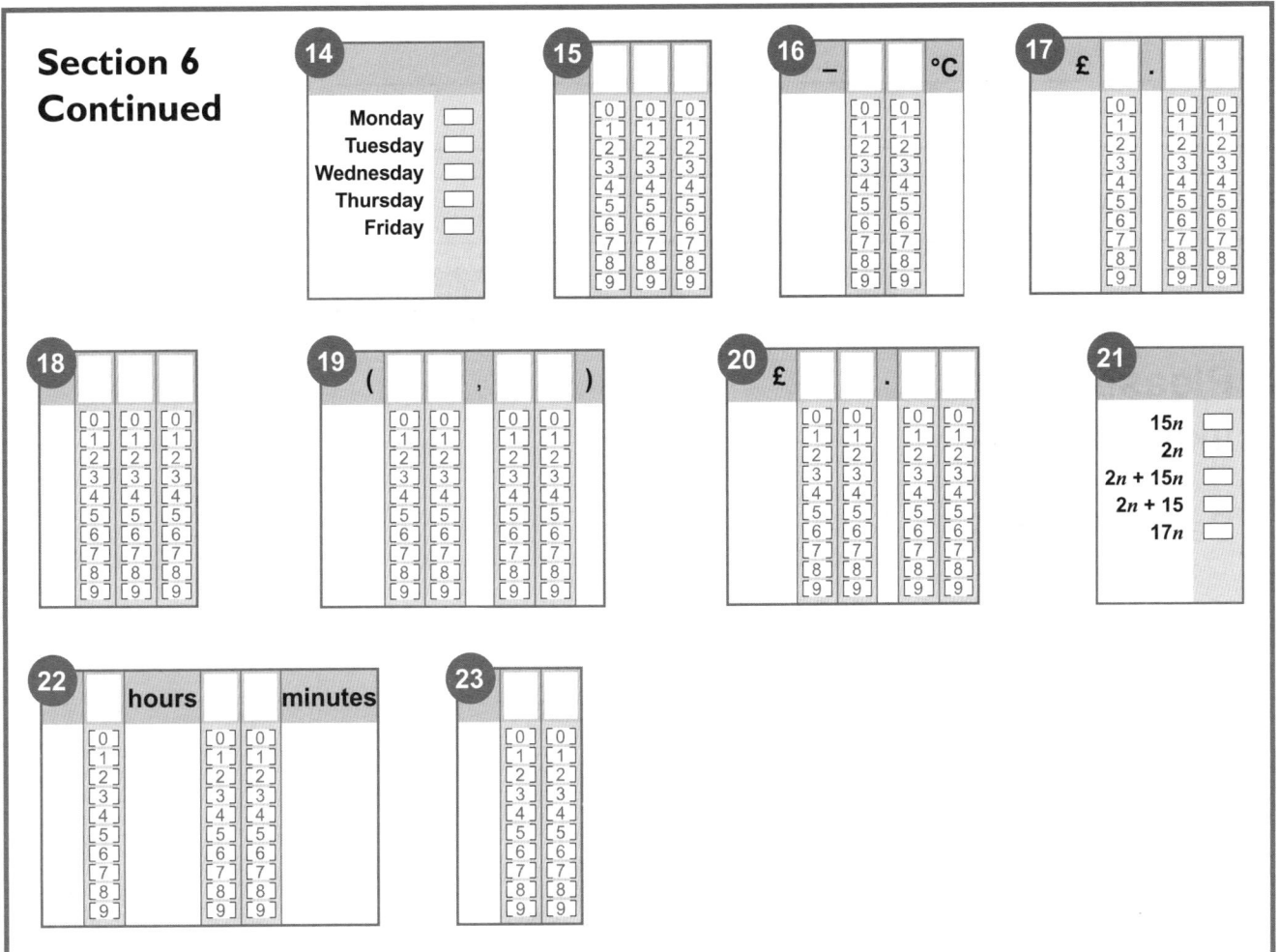

Set A: Paper 2

Pupil's name:

School name:

Test date:

Please mark like this: ⊟

Set A: Paper 2

Pupil Number, School Number, Date of Birth (Day / Month / Year) — bubble grids.

Section 1

EXAMPLE A: Despite / However ⊟ / Also / While

EXAMPLE B: brought / drunk / travelled / arrived ⊟

1. rare / rarest / rarer / rarely
2. exposed / original / related / native
3. considered / admired / resolved / granted
4. misrepresent / define / symbolise / operate
5. reputation / greed / ability / diet
6. experienced / recognised / understood / replicated
7. about / like / for / of
8. appearance / size / strength / charm
9. although / sometimes / therefore / possibly
10. conservation / planting / growth / destruction
11. some / only / almost / over
12. records / recorded / record / recording
13. game / job / role / position
14. disperse / plant / gather / arrange
15. climate / growth / knowledge / colour
16. preserve / diminish / prevent / savour

Section 2

EXAMPLE A1: 6 minutes

EXAMPLE A2: 2 0 m

EXAMPLE A3: speeding up / rising ⊟ / slowing down / falling

1a. ___ m²

1b. 1/14, 1/7, 1/10, 3/14, 2/7

1c. ___ m²

2a.

2b.

2c.

11+ / CEM / 10-11 / 2 / Answer Sheets

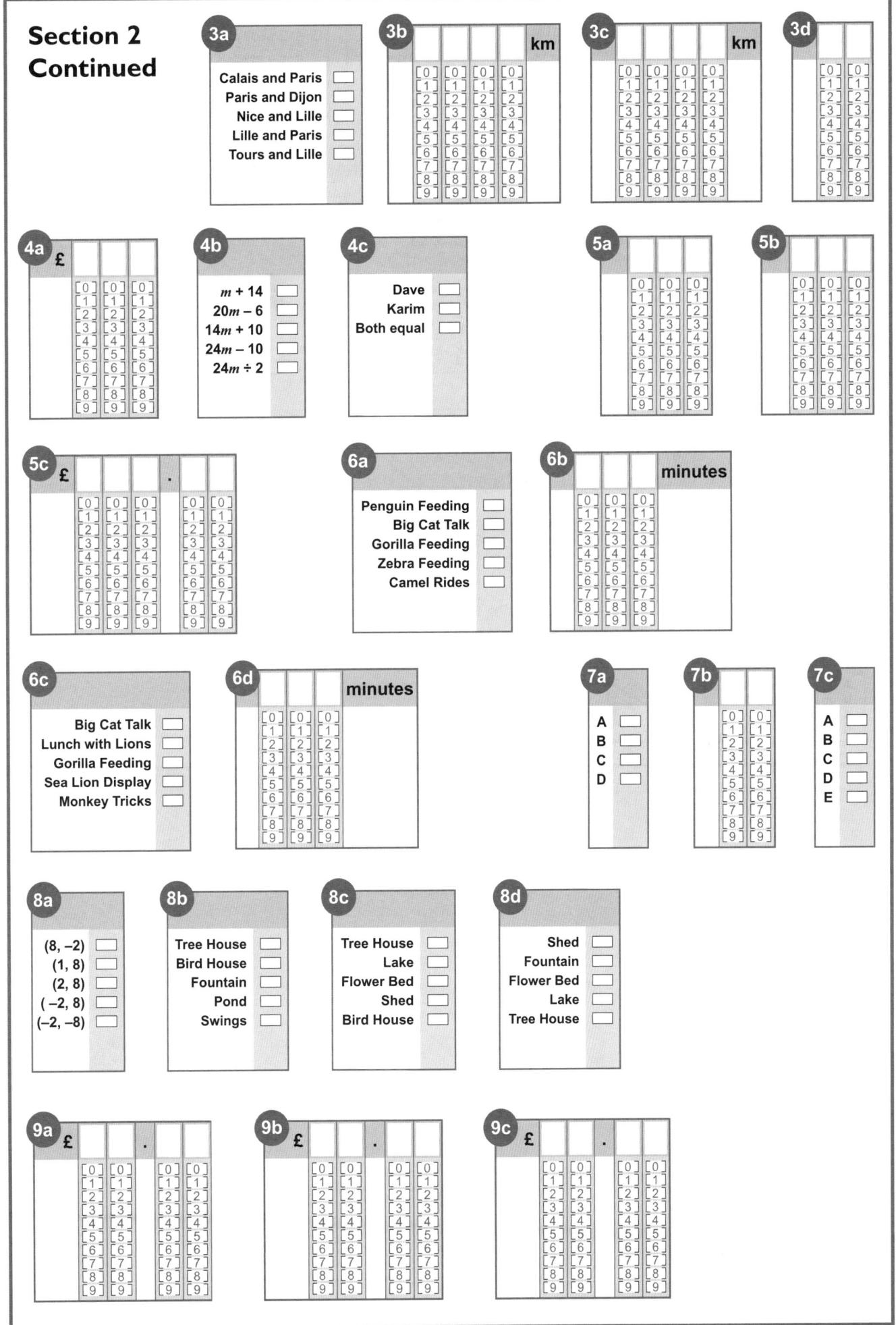

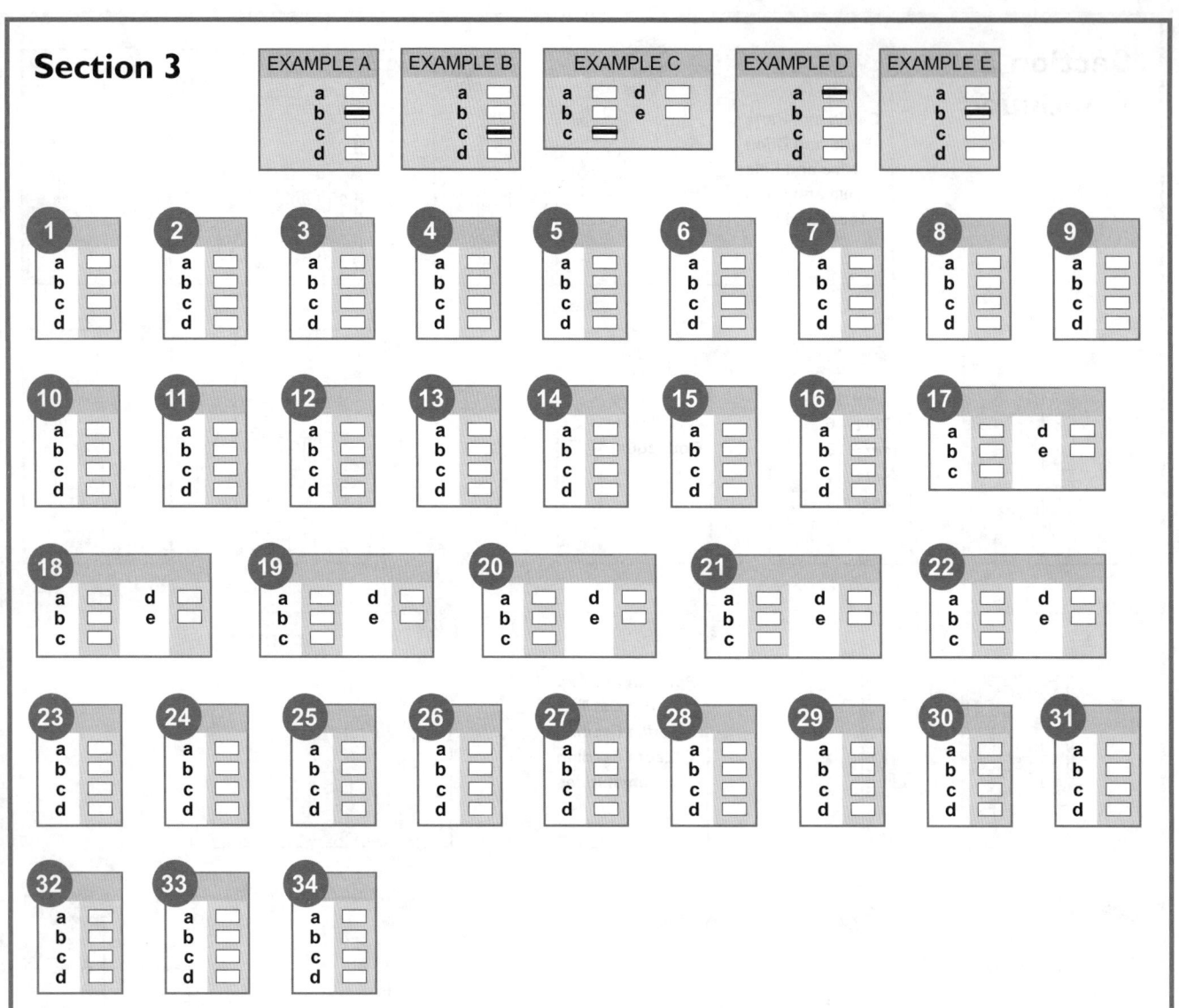

Set B: Paper 1

Pupil's name:

Test date:

School name:

Please mark like this: ▬

Set B: Paper 1

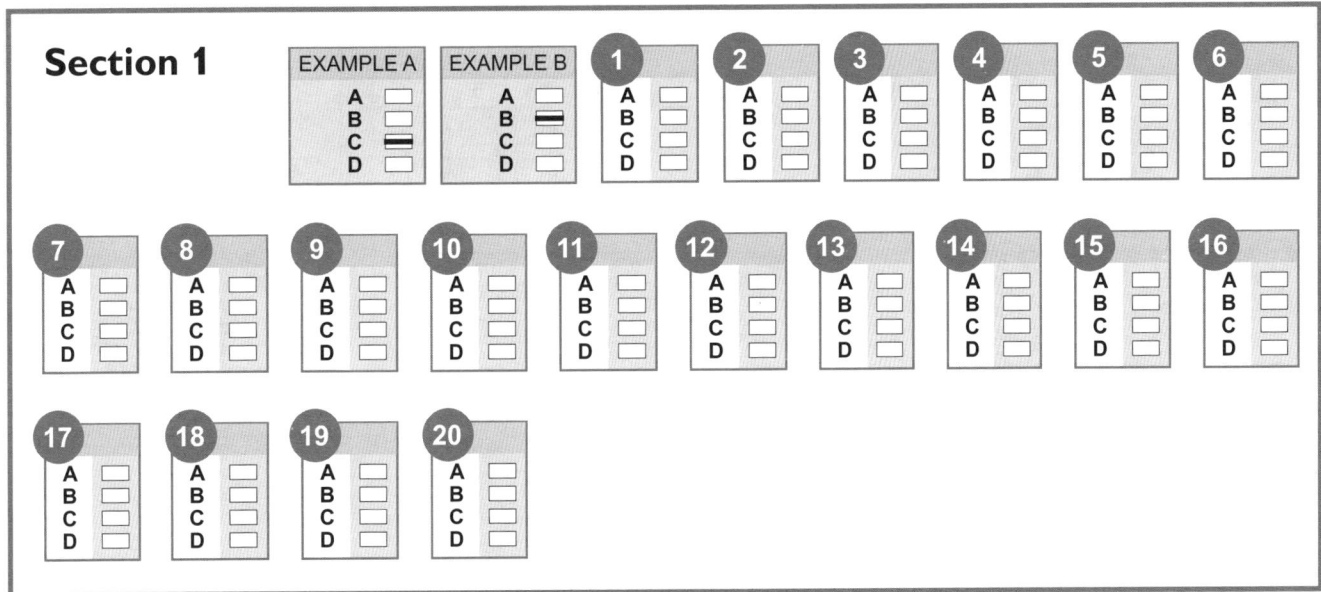

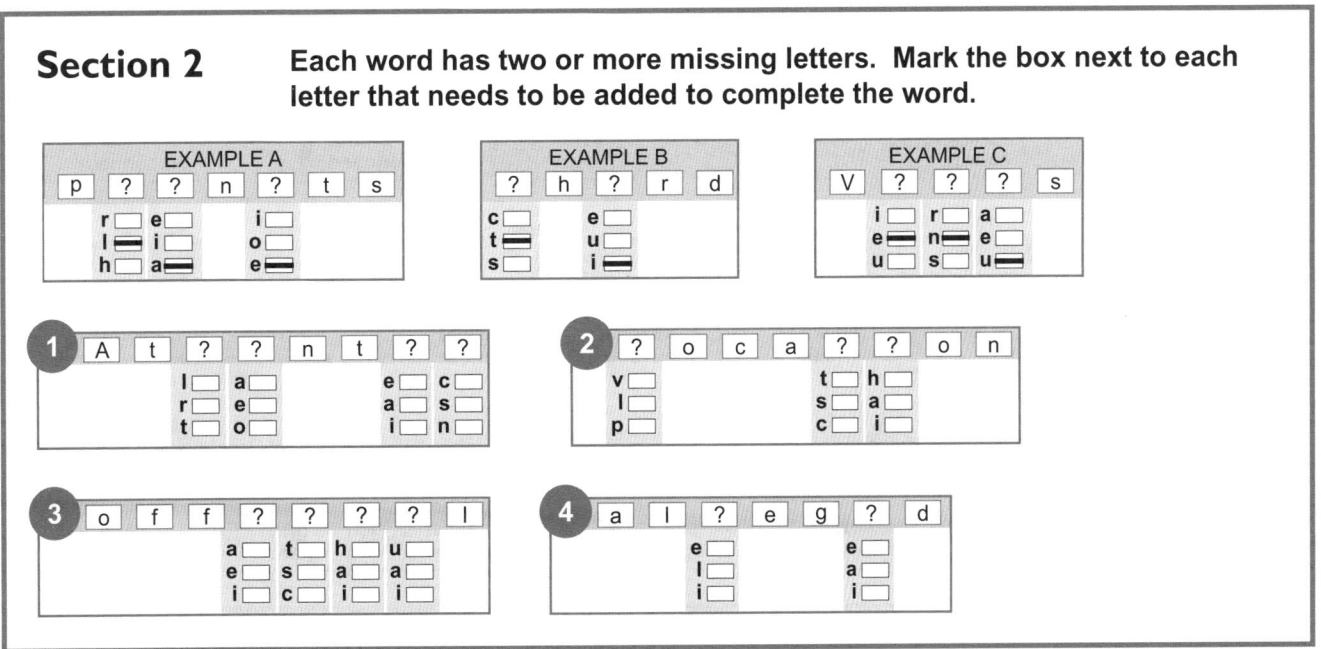

Section 2 Continued

5 b i z ? ? ? e — a/o/n, e/r/g, z/a/r

6 ? e t ? ? e ? n — s/t/i, b/p/e, g/w/a

7 k ? ? ? n — h/o/a/w, l/e/a/w, n/a/r

8 t ? r ? ? t — u/e/a, h/a/r/t

9 s ? o ? ? s — m/r/a, h/t/e, t/v/t

10 p ? ? ? l i a r — i/c/e, a/k/u, r/e/o

11 p l ? ? ? s — a/c/e, o/n/u, e/t/o

12 n ? v ? l — o/e, e/a, a/u

13 v a r ? ? t ? — i/e/e, s/a/y, e/i/s

14 t h e ? r ? ? s — i/i/e, a/y/r, o/r/y

15 ? e ? ? s — f/r/r, t/a/e, y/t/m

16 r a ? i ? n ? l — t/a/e, s/a/e/a, c/o/u

17 b e l ? ? ? e — e/i/e, i/e/i, a/v/v

18 ? ? u s ? d — u/a/e, c/o/e/u, r/n/o

19 ? n ? s ? ? l — k/o/u/e, i/e/u/a, u/u/h/l

20 ? e ? y — r/m, d/l, t/n

21 ? u ? i o ? s — l/r/u, c/n/o, f/s/s

Section 3

EXAMPLE: sister / brother / **family** / cousin

1 draft / chart / table / graph

2 grow / expand / swell / ripe

3 elated / merry / wistful / overjoyed

4 amalgamate / consolidate / blend / disconnect

5 dictionary / encyclopedia / novel / thesaurus

6 aluminium / lead / steel / granite

7 stir / mix / shake / whisk

8 crimson / violet / lilac / mauve

9 butterfly / dragonfly / hornet / moth

10 clasp / buckle / zip / seam

11 classroom / bathroom / bedroom / living room

12 demand / receive / request / ask

13 blurred / pixelated / complicated / obscured

14 birch / oak / rose / sycamore

15 triangle / cube / square / rectangle

16 aunt / grandmother / sister / father

17 scowl / frown / grin / glare

18 dishevelled / awkward / clumsy / inelegant

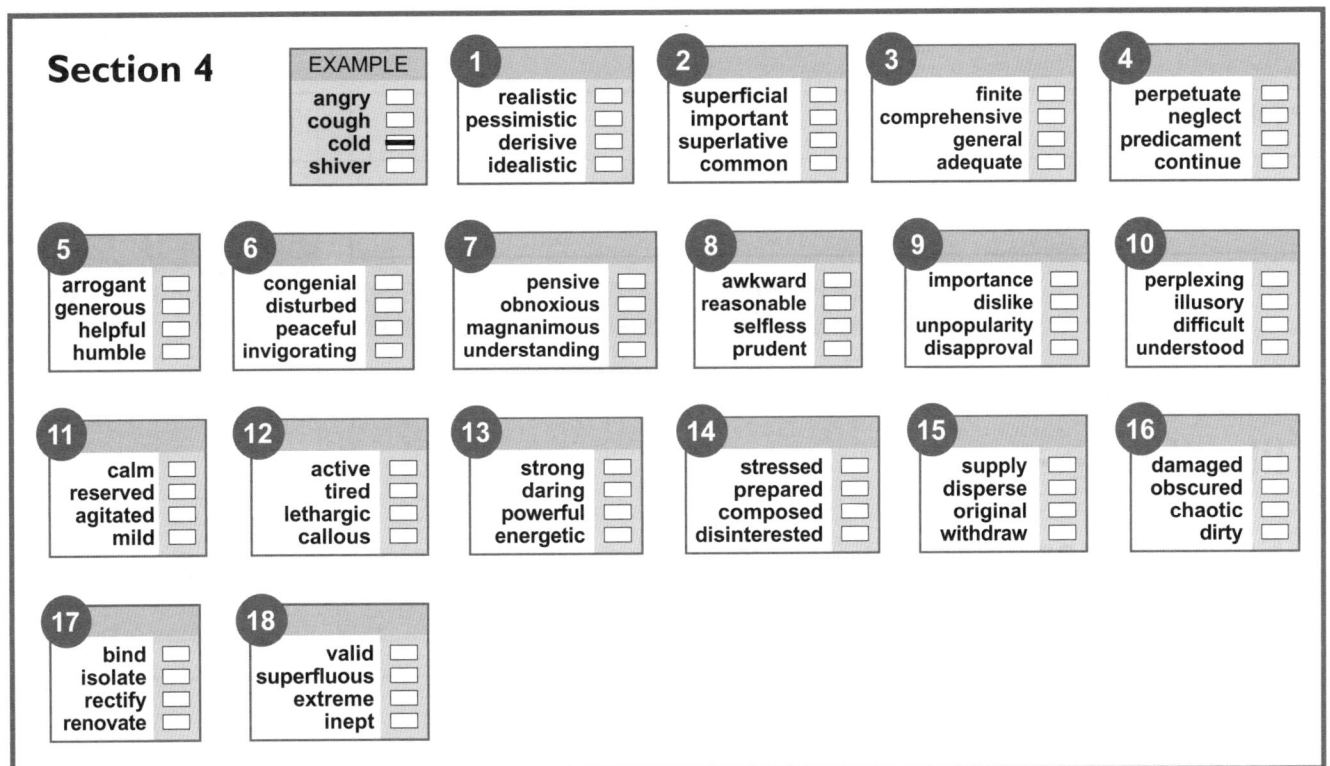
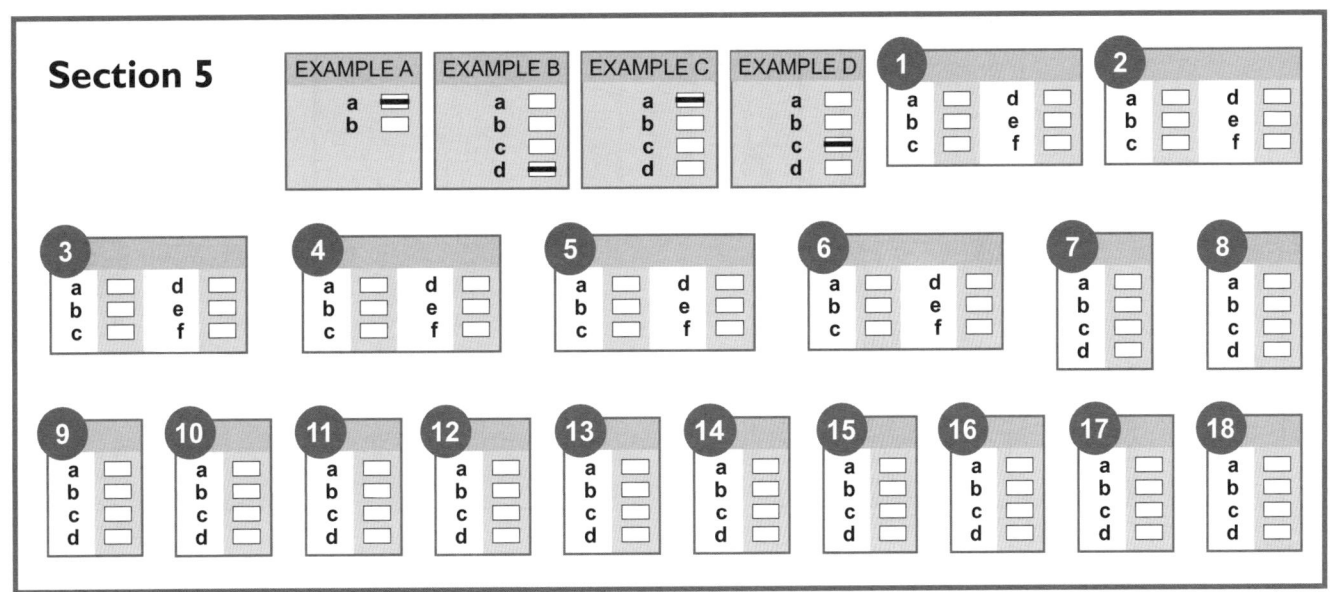

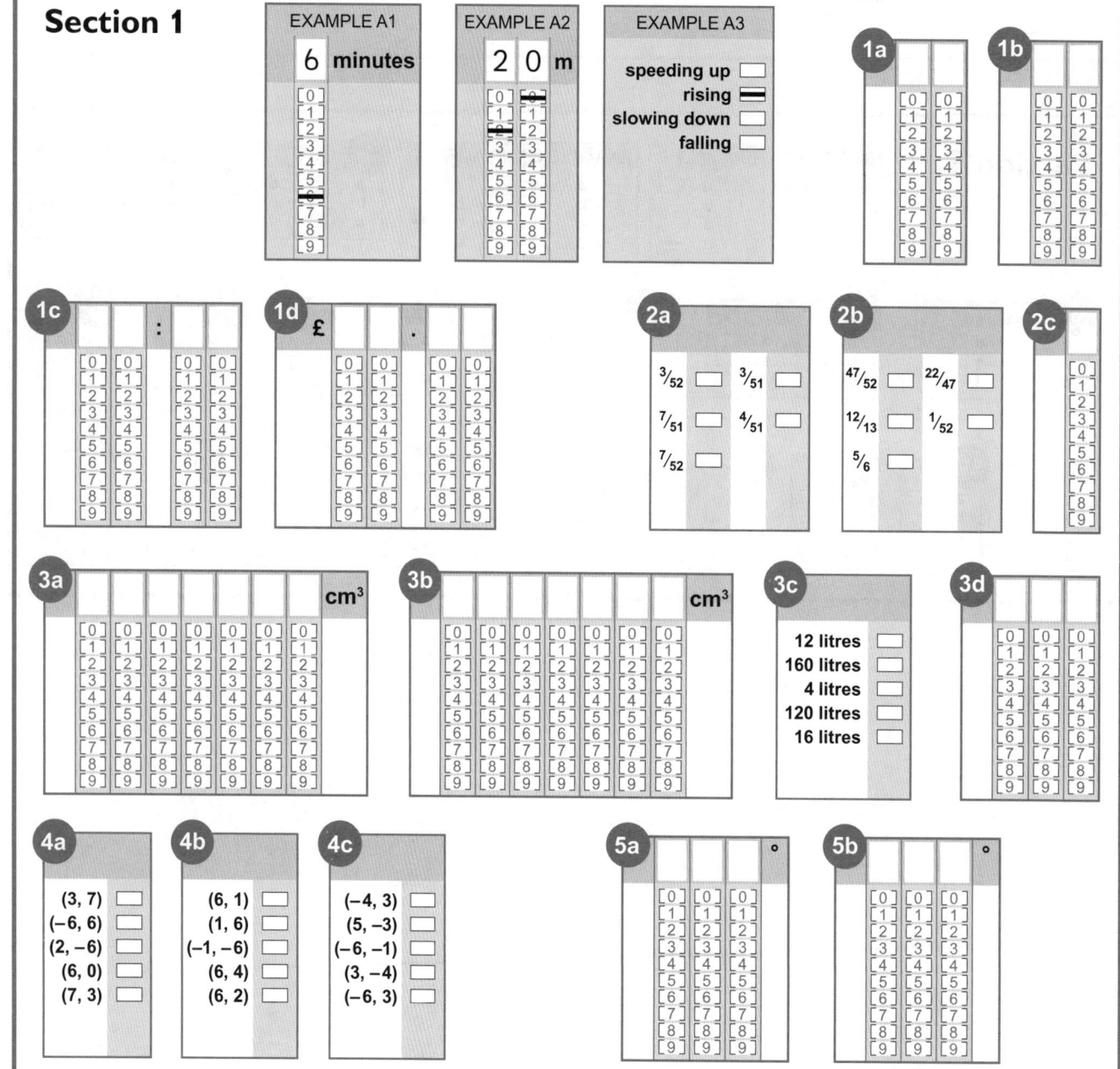

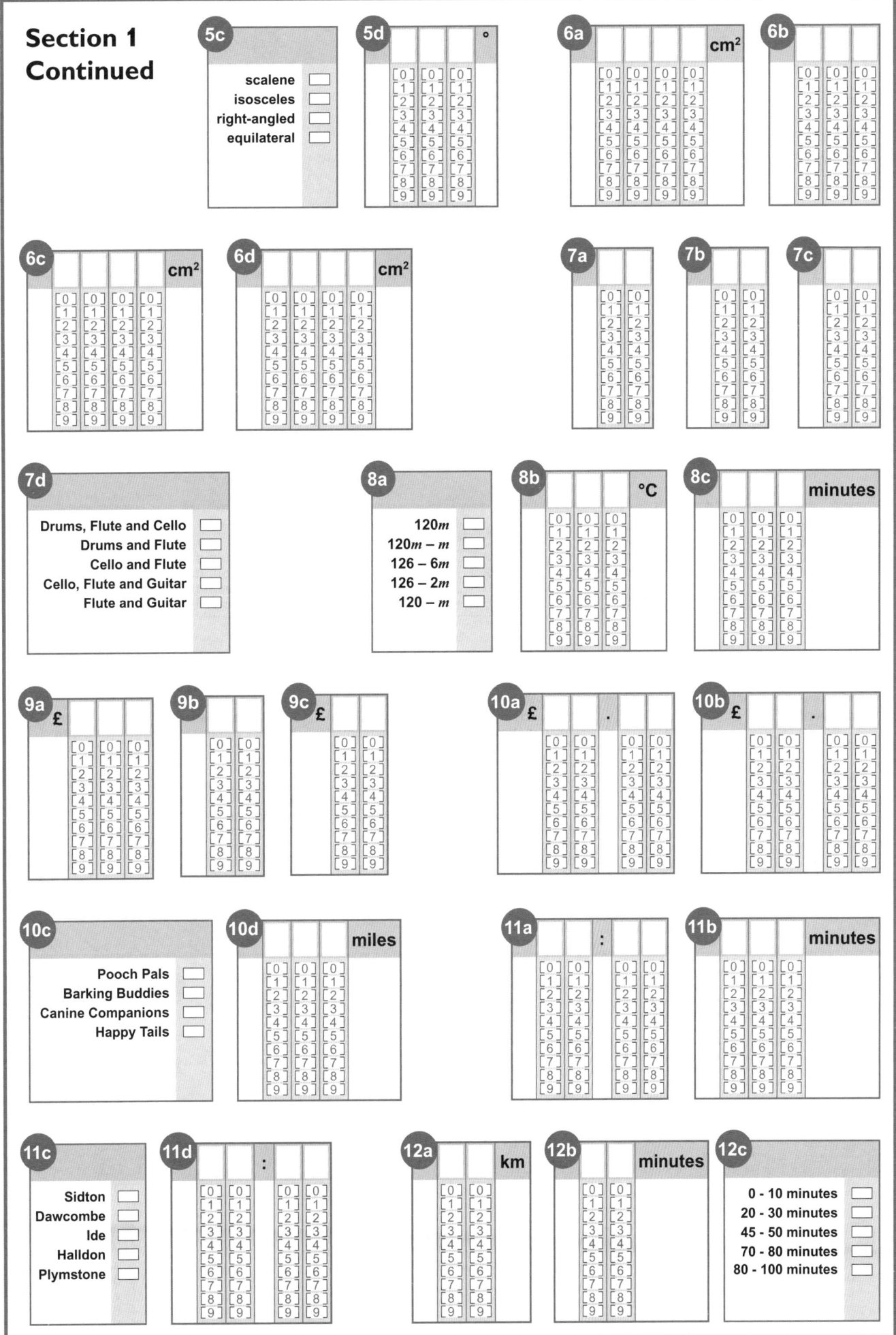

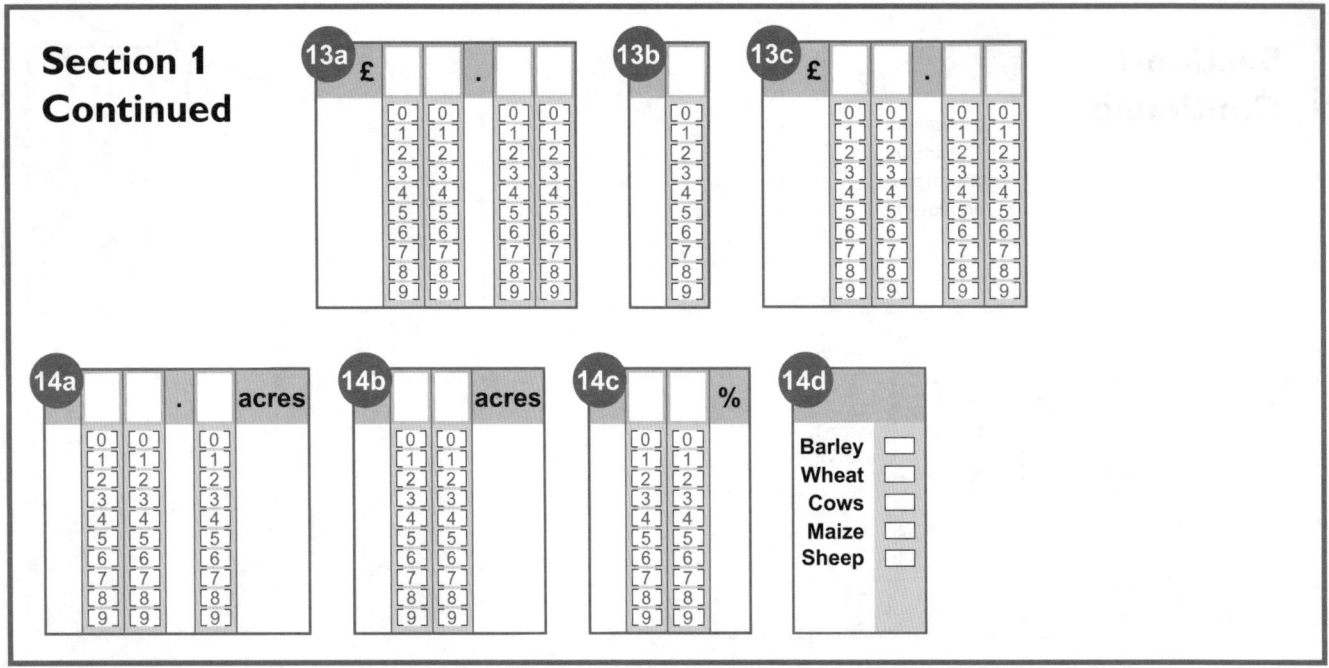
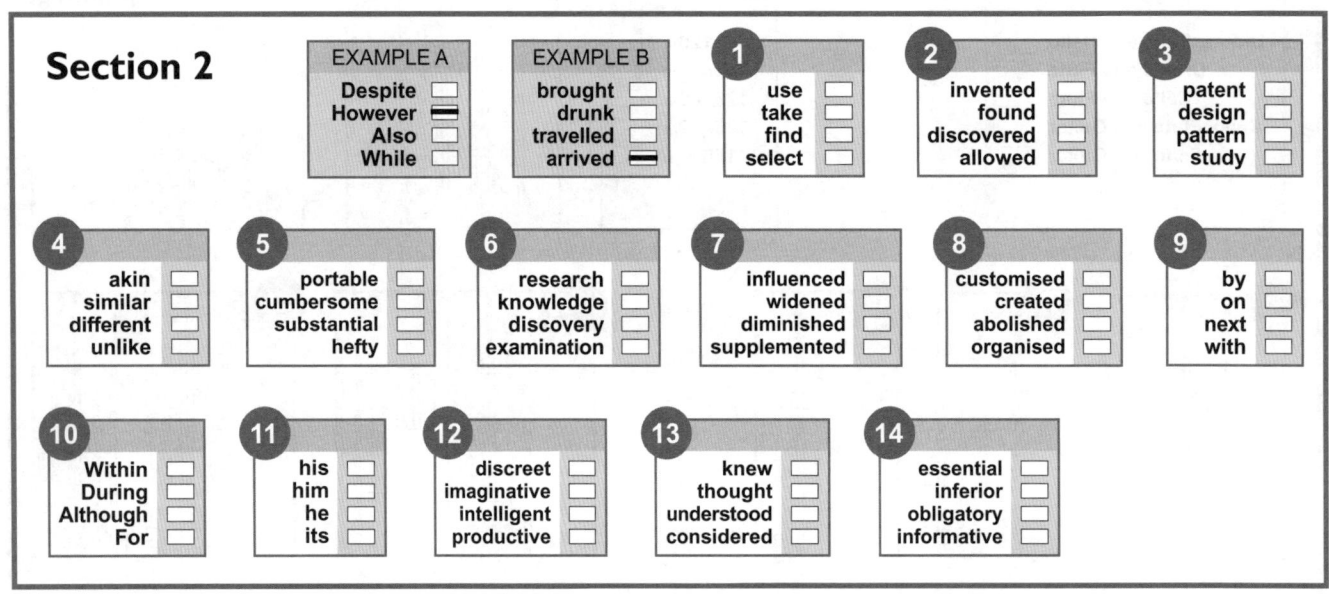
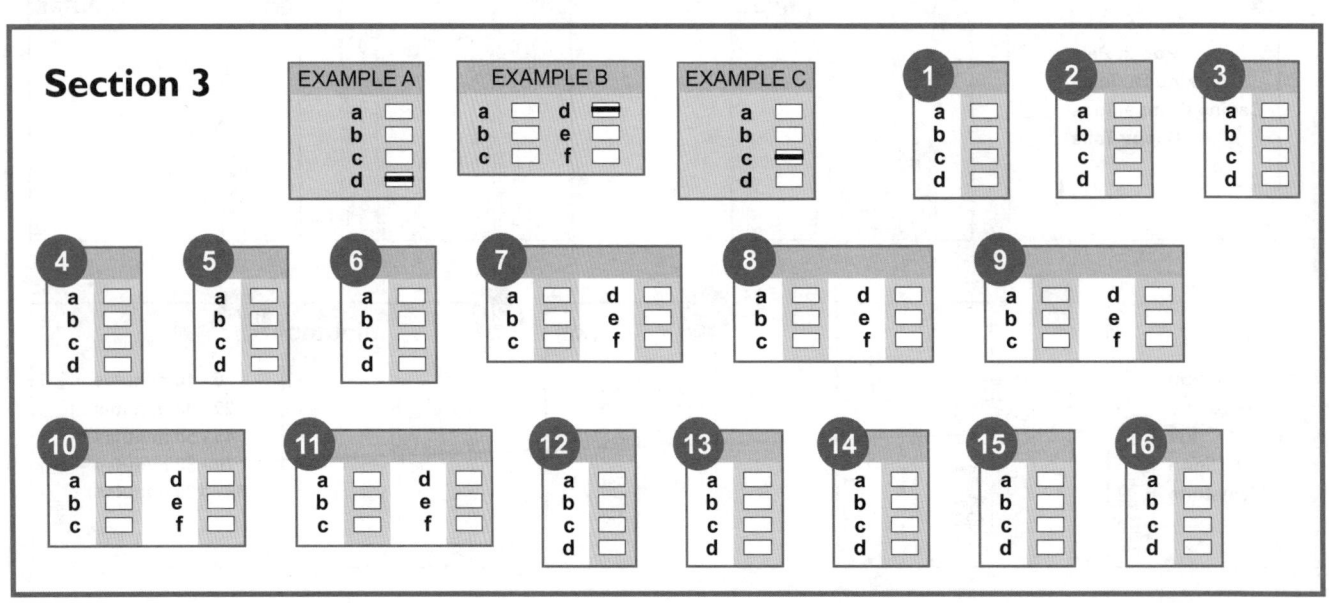

CGP

11+ Practice Papers

For the **CEM** test

Parents' Guide

Ages 10-11

Pack 2

Published by CGP

Editors:
Ben Ffrancon-Davies, Sharon Keeley-Holden, Heather McClelland, Sabrina Robinson, Rebecca Tate, Ben Train, Jonathan Wray

With thanks to Claire Boulter, Paul Jordin and Glenn Rogers for the proofreading.

Please note that CGP is not associated with CEM in any way.
These tests do not include any official questions and they are not endorsed by CEM.

ISBN: 978 1 78908 217 3

Clipart from Corel®
Printed by Elanders Ltd, Newcastle upon Tyne.

Text, design, layout and original illustrations
© Coordination Group Publications Ltd. (CGP) 2018
All rights reserved.

Photocopying more than 5% of a paper is not permitted, even if you have a CLA licence.
Extra copies are available from CGP with next day delivery • 0800 1712 712 • www.cgpbooks.co.uk

What This Pack Contains

What this pack contains

This pack contains **two sets** of 11+ Practice Papers for the CEM test.

The questions in these papers have been written to match the level of difficulty of the real exam. They are designed to test your child's Verbal Reasoning, Comprehension, Non-Verbal Reasoning and Maths skills.

Each of the practice papers in this pack has an accompanying **multiple-choice answer sheet**, just like the answer sheets used in the real 11+ exams. There are also **full answers** to every question in the separate **answer booklet**.

You can also download and play the **online audio instructions**, which are similar to the instructions that your child will hear on test day. (Depending on the format of the test in your area, the instructions could be played as an audio recording, like the ones we have provided, or they may be read aloud by an exam invigilator.)

You can find the audio downloads at:

cgpbooks.co.uk/11plustestaudio

This set of papers also includes a **free Online Edition**. For details of how to access your Online Edition, just follow the instructions in the box below:

How to access your free Online Edition

This book includes a free Online Edition to read on your PC, Mac or tablet.
You'll just need to go to **cgpbooks.co.uk/extras** and enter this code:

3126 1459 5677 5931

By the way, this code only works for one person. If somebody else has used this book before you, they might have already claimed the Online Edition.

The pages that follow in this Parents' Guide are designed to give some guidance and information on how to best prepare for the 11+ test, as well as how to support your child in performing as well as they can.

- It's important to remember that preparing to take the 11+ can be a stressful time for both parents and pupils. You should do all you can to minimise pressure for the whole family, and try to make the whole process as positive an experience as possible.
- When studying for the 11+, your child will learn plenty of new skills that can have a beneficial impact on their whole education, regardless of whether they pass the 11+ test.
- With the right mindset and preparation, your child will be able to approach the test with confidence, and come out of it feeling positive about their performance.

What is the 11+?

It can be tricky to find reliable information about the 11+ and how to prepare for it. This page covers the basics — what the 11+ test is and how it works.

The 11+ is a selective test

Most secondary schools in the UK are comprehensive — they're non-selective and accept children of all abilities. But in some areas, selective state secondary schools (grammar schools) still exist. These schools select their pupils based on academic ability.

The 11+ test is used to determine if a child is suitable for grammar school. It's also used for entry to some independent schools. Children usually sit the test in the first term of their last year at primary school.

Some schools select pupils based just on the 11+ test results, but others look at other factors, e.g. whether you live close to the school, or if you have other children at the school.

The format of the test varies

The exact format of the 11+ test varies depending on the school or Local Authority (LA) you're applying to, as well as on the provider that sets the test. There are two main test providers for the 11+ — **GL Assessment** and **CEM**. However, in some cases, the test papers will be written by the school, or by a consortium of schools in that area.

Make sure you know which of these providers is responsible for the test in your area, and find out as much information as you can about the format of the test before you start.

Wherever you are, there are four main subjects that can be tested:

> **Verbal Reasoning** — problem-solving and logic using words, letters, numbers, etc.
> **Non-Verbal Reasoning** — problem-solving and logic using pictures and symbols.
> **Maths** — often at the same level as the SATs, but it may be more challenging.
> **English** — reading comprehension, grammar and sometimes a writing task.

Tests set by GL Assessment can include any combination of these four subjects (you won't necessarily have to do all four). Traditionally, there would be a different test paper for each subject — however, some GL regions now have mixed papers, with two papers that each cover more than one subject. Check the format of the test in your region well in advance of test day.

Papers set by CEM are usually mixed, and will cover Verbal Reasoning, Non-Verbal Reasoning and Maths. However, CEM Verbal Reasoning does contain some of the same elements as GL English, such as comprehension.

The tests are usually either **multiple choice** (MC) or **standard answer** (SA) format.

> **Multiple choice** — there's a separate answer sheet. There's usually a choice of five options for each answer, and the answers may be computer-marked.
> **Standard answer** — there are spaces on the question paper for the pupil to write their own answers. There will usually not be any answer options given for the pupil to choose from.

Using the Practice Papers

This advice will help you to get the most out of this set of practice papers. You may wish to administer the practice papers in exam conditions to help your child become familiar with the format of the test.

These practice papers are in multiple-choice format

There is advice on filling in the multiple-choice answer sheets on page 3 of the answer sheet booklet. Read through this advice with your child before you begin. Make sure that they understand what they need to do before they begin a paper, and that they are filling in the answer sheet which matches the paper they are attempting.

How to set the practice papers

- Do the practice papers at a time when your child usually works well. This might be a weekday after school, or at the weekend. This will help them work to the best of their abilities.
- As you get closer to the actual test, it is a good idea to sit some practice papers at the same time of day as the real thing — that way, your child will be used to the routine and there shouldn't be any surprises.
- Your child should attempt the practice paper at a clear table in a quiet area, free from distractions and interruptions.
- They'll need a sharp pencil, an eraser and a pencil sharpener.
- You can play the online audio to mimic real exam conditions. The audio runs through the instructions found on the front of the practice paper, and will give your child information about timings.
- If you're not using the online audio instructions, read out the instructions on the front of the practice paper before your child begins. Make sure that they understand what they have to do. Position your child so they can see a watch or clock so that they can keep track of the time they have left.
- Time the test strictly. If they haven't finished the paper in the time allowed, you could draw a line under the last question they answered within the time limit so you know to give marks up to that point. You can then time them to see how long it takes them to finish the paper. This will allow you to monitor the speed your child is working at.
- Encourage them to read over their answers if they finish within the time limit, but don't give them extra time to do this.
- Mark their test using the answers in the separate answer booklet.

Marking the practice papers

You should give one mark for each correct answer your child gave within the time limit, then work out the total score. It's really important to go through any wrong answers with your child — use the explanations in the answer book to show them how to find the right answer.

The pass mark will vary from school to school and year to year. It's common practice for your child's 'raw score' (i.e. the actual number of questions they answered correctly) to be converted into a 'standardised score'. This helps to make the results fairer by taking your child's age into account, as well as bringing scores for different papers in line with each other. As such, there is no number of correct answers that will guarantee a pass, but for these practice papers, we suggest that your child aims for a score of 85% or more.

Your child's score might help you pinpoint specific skills that they need to practise. For example, if your child scored 60%, got nearly all the questions right, but didn't finish the test, they need to work faster. We have given some advice to help you increase your child's speed on p.6.

If they scored 60%, got to the end, but got 40% of the questions wrong, they need to brush up on their accuracy. You can follow this up with some more practice in the areas they struggled with, then set another practice test.

Improving Your Child's Score

For your child to do well in their 11+, they'll need to work quickly and avoid making mistakes. Here's some advice to help improve your child's score and test technique.

Start by working on accuracy...

When your child is just starting out, it's a good idea to focus on their accuracy and understanding, rather than speed. You can work on their speed when they're a bit more confident.

Once your child has finished a paper and you've marked it, you should go over the questions they got wrong, so they know how they should have answered them. You could even come back to these trickier questions at a later date to make sure they can still get them right.

...then work on speed

In the real 11+ test, children are deliberately put under time pressure. This helps schools distinguish between good candidates and the best ones. The faster your child is, the more questions they'll answer. Once your child can accurately answer 11+ questions, use these tips to help them improve their speed:

- Find out the timings of the real test — how long your child will have, and how many questions they'll have to answer. When they're practising, give them slightly less time than this to do the same number of questions.
- Encourage your child only to check their answers if they have time at the end of the test.
- You could introduce games to get them working faster — try using a stopwatch to time a set of questions, and get your child to ring a bell or shout when they've finished them.
- For comprehension questions, it's important that your child can read the text quickly. Encourage them to read the text first, then look at the questions — remind them that they can look back at the text as many times as they like when answering the questions.

In the run-up to the test, start working on test technique

Your child will score better on the 11+ if they improve their test technique. Good test technique is also important for their SATs, and other exams later in their education. When they start working through assessment papers, remind them to do the following things:

- Read the front of the paper and enter the correct information on it.
- Skip any questions that are really difficult, or which are taking a long time — they can come back to them if there's time at the end.
- If they can't do a question and they're running out of time, make a sensible guess. For multiple-choice questions, they may be able to rule out one or two options that definitely aren't correct, which gives a better chance of guessing which of the remaining ones is right.

If your child's test is in multiple-choice format, there are some other specific techniques to practise:

- Marking the correct box neatly and quickly using a horizontal line.
- Making sure they mark the answer in the correct box, especially if they skip a question.
- If they don't finish the paper, filling in the rest of the answers randomly.

When your child does a practice paper, they should work in silence and without help. Try to make their experience as close to the real test as possible.

What to Expect on Test Day

The test day and the time before you get the results can be just as stressful for you as for your child. Here are some tips about how to reduce this stress, and how to cope with the waiting period.

Facing the test

Make sure you and your child are fully prepared for the day of the test. You need to know:

- Where the test is and how you're going to get there (parking may be difficult).
- What time the test starts and what time you need to arrive by.
- What they'll need to take (pencils, etc.) or whether everything is provided for them.

Make sure your child is as relaxed as possible the night before the test, and that they get a good night's sleep. A healthy evening meal and breakfast before the test will also help put your child in the right frame of mind to tackle the test. It's also a good idea to talk them through the arrangements for the day so they know what will happen.

After the test, plan an outing or a treat which will take your child's (and your) mind off the test. Even if your child is still preparing for other 11+ tests, they'll need a break.

- There's usually a retest day for children who are ill on the day of the test. Check with the school in advance, and let the test centre know as soon as possible if you can't make it to the test.
- If you think there are circumstances that have affected your child's performance in the test, gather evidence of this as soon as possible (e.g. a doctor's note or school marks that have dipped). Once you've got the results it'll be too late.

After the 11+

Make a plan for the time between the last of your child's tests and the day you get their results — this wait can be very stressful.

If you're going to reward your child for their hard work preparing for the 11+, you might want to do it now. If they're rewarded for their effort and hard work, they'll realise that they've achieved something, even if their results aren't what they hoped for.

Remind your child that you are proud of them no matter what the outcome, and try not to build up results day as too big a deal. If your child is unsuccessful, then it's not the end of the world. If your child does gain a grammar school place, then make sure they're aware that some of their classmates might not have done, and may need a friend to help make them feel better.

If you feel there is good reason, then this is also a good time to research the appeals process for the schools you've applied to. Some parents choose to appeal the admission decision if their child isn't offered a place.

Make sure you have an alternative plan

For some grammar schools, there can be several applicants for each available place. Even if your child scores highly on the test, it may still not be enough to gain a place at the school. You should put at least one non-selective school on your secondary school application form — it's a good idea to have visited these schools, so your child knows what to expect if they aren't offered a grammar school place.

It's important that your child doesn't feel like a failure if they don't get into a grammar school — there are many excellent comprehensive schools where your child can be happy and successful. Remember that school is what you make it, and a positive response to not gaining a grammar school place is key to this.